The AD 70 Doctrine
Realized Eschatology

By Morris G. Bowers

Doctrinal Implications of
Preterist Eschatology
versus what the Holy Spirit has
revealed in the Bible

© 2009 Spiritbuilding Publishing. All rights reserved. No part of this book may be reproduced in any form without the written permission of the publisher.

Published by
Spiritbuilding Publishing
15591 N. State Rd. 9, Summitville, IN 46070

Spiritual "equipment" for the contest of life.
Printed in the United States of America

Bowers, Morris G.
    The AD 70 Doctrine: Realized Eschatology
    ISBN 9780982137673

The New King James Version,© 1982 by Thomas Nelson, Inc. Used by permission. All rights reserved. *The New American Standard Bible,*©1960-1977, 1995 by the Lockman Foundation. Used by permission.

Young's Literal Translation: The Bible text designated YLT is from the 1898 *Young's Literal Translation* by Robert Young who also compiled Young's Analytical Concordance. This is an extremely literal translation that attempts to preserve the tense and word usage as found in the original Greek and Hebrew writings. The text was scanned from a reprint of the 1898 edition as published by Baker Book House, Grand Rapids Michigan. The book is still in print and may be ordered from Baker Book House. Obvious errors in spelling or inconsistent spellings of the same word were corrected in the computer edition of the text.

Publisher

Gospel Themes Press
2028 South Austin Street Suite 906
Amarillo, TX 79109-1960, USA

www.spiritbuilding.com

Also by Morris G. Bowers

ISRAEL the 51st State...the Unspoken Foreign Policy of the United State of America, published by iUniverse, 2005, www.iuniverse.com, www.amazon.com

Secular Humanism...the Official Religion of the United States of America, published by .PublishAmerica, Baltimore, 2007, www.PublishAmerica.com, www.amazon.com

The Search...for the Church that Christ Built, Matthew 16:18, Published by Sable Publishing House, London, England, 2008, www.Sable-Publishing-House.com, www.amazon.uk.com

To my Mother and Father, (deceased)
The nicest, smartest, and most moral parents possible!

Table of Contents

	PAGE
Preface	1
Introduction	5
Chapter 1 - Reviewing The Parousia	8
Chapter 2 - The Second Coming of Christ, the Resurrection and the Judgment--Their Timing and Nature	22
Chapter 3 - Doctrinal Implications of Preterist Eschatology	35
Chapter 4 - Matthew 24 Explained	48
Chapter 5 - The Preterist View Heresy	67
Chapter 6 - The A.D. 70 System of Kingism (The Church)	100
Chapter 7 - The Second Coming of Christ: Did it Already Occur?	120
Chapter 8 - Haunting Questions Regarding Realized Eschatology and the A.D. 70 Doctrine	138
Chapter 9 - The Judge of All	151
End Notes and Additional Info	160

Important Note:
Articles in this manuscript come from a number of different sources. In order to faithfully preserve the article, punctuation and much of the formatting has been left as is. Even when we wished to correct it, the formatting has been faithfully reproduced. Spiritbuilding publishing accepts no responsibility for these reproduced errors.

Men never do evil so completely and cheerfully as when they do it from a religious conviction.

- Blaise Pascal

Preface

Every generation faces the challenge to understand and apply the Bible for themselves. No one should blindly accept what previous generations have taught just because of past practices. Those who know the Lord will learn to search "the Scriptures daily *to find out* whether these things were so" (Acts 17:11). Those who refuse to examine past practices by an open Bible are indeed caught up in a loyalty to a human tradition above God (Matthew 15:8-9). It is my goal for this book to encourage such a discussion.

Also with every generation, a movement arises that carries the banner of opposing the plain and simple teachings of the "God Breathed" Scripture that we have revealed in the Bible and having the desire to see "radical" changes within the church. There is a real danger for those who seek reform to actually form a human movement with human loyalties that are forming new human traditions to contrast with the practices they oppose. When this happens you will often find a group of doctrinal positions taken that will define the new movement. There then will be an effort made to line people up through name-calling, peer-pressure, and other carnal weapons. When this occurs, pride, bitterness, and a desire for control of others motivate these "reformers." Division occurs in these settings and another sect is born. Please carefully look into your heart and of those who are seeking reform to be sure that you have a heart of love and an open Bible rather than the "win at all costs" attitude of one who will slander and destroy others just to add another slave to a new human movement (Galatians 4:17-20; 2 Peter 2:19).

The above theory is not a new or fresh approach to Scripture, but is actually a retelling of an old error. In 1883, Dr. A. Wilford Hall wrote a book entitled, *Universalism Against Itself.* The author noted, "Universalism teaches that this important event (the coming of Christ) took place at the destruction of Jerusalem, 2000 years ago. This position is taken in order to avoid, if possible, the admission of a future general judgment, which every where stands closely connected with the second coming of Christ" *(p. 91)*. In fact, in the 1930's, C.H. Dodd taught a similar error (the final events were all fulfilled in the personal ministry of Jesus) and gave it the name, "Realized Eschatology."

Because there are some passages in which Jesus is described *as "coming" in a local or physical judgment* upon Jerusalem *(Matthew 24:1-34)*, some erroneously contend that all New Testament references to the *"coming" of Christ in judgment must allude to the destruction of Jerusalem*. This contention ignores the fact that the Scriptures portray Jesus as "coming" in a number of different senses. 1. Jesus "came" to earth as a human being *(Luke 19:10)*. 2. He "came" when the church was established on Pentecost *(Matthew 16:28; Mark 9:1)*. 3. He "comes" to discipline congregations that are no longer faithful *(Revelation 2:5)*. 4. In addition, He has promised to "come" in a universal judgment *(Matthew 25:31-32)*.

This book is simply an appeal to God fearing people to hold fast to the word of God as it is written, to be not led away by human theories that contradict God's word or distort it. It is God breathed!

Did all of these things happen in AD 70?
1. Acts 1:11, "and they also said, "Men of Galilee, why do you stand looking into the sky? This Jesus, who has been taken up from you into heaven, will come in just the same way as you have watched Him go into heaven." NASB
2. John 5:28-29, "Do not marvel at this; for an hour is coming, in which all who are in the tombs shall hear His voice, and shall come forth; those who did the good deeds to a resurrection of life, those who committed the evil deeds to a resurrection of judgment." NASB
3. 2 Peter 3:10-13, "But the day of the Lord will come like a thief, in which the heavens will pass away with a roar and the elements will be destroyed with intense heat, and the earth and its works will be burned up. Since all these things are to be destroyed in this way, what sort of people ought you to be in holy conduct and godliness, looking for and hastening the coming of the day of God, on account of which the heavens will be destroyed by burning, and the elements will melt with intense heat! But according to His promise we are looking for new heavens and a new earth, in which righteousness dwells." NASB
4. Revelation 22:12-14, "Behold, I am coming quickly, and My reward is with Me, to render to every man according to what he has done. "I am the Alpha and the Omega, the first and the last, the beginning and the end." Blessed are those who wash their robes, that they may have the right to the tree of life, and may enter by the gates into the city."[1] NASB

Radical preterism (also known as "realized eschatology" or the "A.D. 70 doctrine") is so "off the wall"—biblically speaking—that one wonders how anyone ever falls for it. But they do. And as exasperating as it is, the doctrine needs to be addressed from time to time. One writer, in reviewing the A.D. 70 heresy, recently quipped that dealing with preterism is like cleaning the kitty litter box; one hates to fool with it, but it has to be done. He can just be thankful that cats aren't larger than they are.

Preterists strive for consistency in their view of Bible prophecy. The goal is admirable. But when a series of propositions is linked, and they are grounded on the same faulty foundation, when one of them topples—like dominos in a line—they all fall. So it is with the A.D. 70 theory.

Here is the problem. In studying the New Testament material relative to the "coming" of Christ, preterists note that:

1. There are passages which seem to speak of the nearness of the Lord's coming—from a first-century vantage point (cf. James 5:8);

2. They observe that there are texts which indicate a "coming" in connection with the destruction of Jerusalem in A.D. 70 (cf. Matthew 24:30);

3. Combining these, they conclude that the Savior's "second coming" must have transpired in A.D. 70; and

4. Furthermore, since the Scriptures are clear as to the fact that the resurrection of the dead, the judgment day, and the end of the world will all occur on the day the Lord returns, the advocates of realized eschatology are forced to "spiritualize" these several happenings, contending that all will take place at the same time. In this "interpretive" process, a whole host of biblical terms must be redefined in order to make them fit the scheme.

And so, while preterists attempt to be consistent, it is nonetheless a sad reality that they are consistently wrong!

---

[1] Olan Hicks, The AD 70 Theory of Last Things

A major fallacy of the preterist mentality is a failure to recognize the elasticity of chronological jargon within the context of biblical prophecy. It is a rather common trait in prophetic language that an event, while literally in the remote future, may be described as near. The purpose in this sort of language is to emphasize the certainty of the prophecy's fulfillment.

There are numerous prophecies of this nature, including passages like James 5:8—"the coming of the Lord is at hand." James could not have been predicting the literally imminent return of the Savior, for such knowledge was not made available to the Lord's penmen. Not even Jesus himself knew of the time of His return to earth (Matthew 24:36, *"But of that day and hour no one knows, not even the angels of heaven, nor the Son, but the Father alone."*)[2]

There are serious problems with the teaching of this doctrine. A few are mentioned below and we will examine these and more as we develop this document.

1. Baptism is paralleled to the resurrection of Christ *(Romans 6:3-5)*, but seeing that the resurrection is supposedly past, does baptism have any validity?
2. The Lord's Supper was to be observed *until He comes (1 Corinthians 11:26)*, but *if He has come*, then where is the authority to continue to partake?
3. Jesus said concerning the resurrection of the dead that they, *"neither marry, nor are given in marriage" (Luke 20:35)*. If the resurrection has already happened, then Christians do not have the right to marry.
4. Jesus also noted that after the resurrection, *"neither can they die anymore" (Luke 20:35)*. If this is not literal, then it is spiritual, and if that is the case then the A.D. 70 advocates have Jesus teaching that no Christian can fall away after the destruction of Jerusalem. In closing, these people have joined Hymenaeus and Philetus in affirming that the resurrection is past already *(2 Timothy 2:16-19).*[3]

As we continue our search and exposure of this false doctrine that has up

---

[2] Jackson, Wayne. 2005. *The A.D. 70 Theory*. Stockton, CA: Christian Courier Publications and Sproul, R. C. 1999. *The Christian News*, June 7.

[3] Mark Dunagan/Beaverton Church of Christ/503-644-9017

set so many Christians lately, I will do my best to give you book, chapter, and verse for everything that I say about their teaching. I have given all diligence to let Scripture interpret Scripture, and at the same time avoid any misuse of Scripture. Some prophecies are admittedly difficult, but allowing the Scriptures to naturally unfold their meaning, I believe I follow the safest approach in reaching truth. [empasis mgb]

Introduction

Because of the serious effect this heresy has had upon individuals and entire churches, it is necessary that it be exposed for what it is - *a perversion of the gospel of Christ. It is not a harmless, private conviction which can be held without hurting oneself and others, but a pernicious theory of error which engulfs the soul of men in destructive heresy.* "The time to inform our people on this subject is now, while it is a simple matter of teaching them on the issues involved. But if we wait, then we may awake one of these days to find ourselves fighting this issue in our own backyards and congregations . . ." I do not say this to criticize any brother, preacher, or church for becoming concerned now rather than sooner. I am pointing this out in an effort to convince any who may continue to be skeptics that we need for you to rise up and help face down this plague. The doctrine known primarily as the A.D. 70 doctrine is completely false from top to bottom. It denies the truth of God's word and it damns the souls of those who embrace it. Furthermore, no congregation who loves and respects the truth and integrity of Scripture can in any way, shape, matter, or form offer, in the slightest, any fellowship to the doctrine or to those who hold to it.

Changing the Lord's Church

In order for change agents to accomplish their goals, they must deconstruct the language, motives, and parameters of the kingdom of Christ and convince others to incorporate their new reality.

They must change the thoughts of their brethren at their outset by altering the way Scripture is understood. Traditional hermeneutics must be discredited and replaced with a more malleable method. Once accomplished, the church can be steered toward their desired goal.

In the Garden of Eden, Satan approaches Eve and incites her to violate God's will by eating of the forbidden fruit of the tree of the knowledge of good and evil. He makes three propositions and convinces her to sin. Subsequently Adam sins and they are expelled from the Garden (Genesis 3).

"Now the serpent was more cunning than any beast of the field..." (Genesis 3:1, NKJV). Wisely, Satan presented truth to Eve interspersed with enough error to lead her astray. The right excised or added word can lead to wholly different results.

God said, "you shall surely die" (Genesis 2:17). Satan cooed that God said they would "not surely die" (Genesis 3:4). God meant spiritual death while Satan likely referred to physical death. His subtle change was designed to create doubt in the mind of Eve.

Satan's deception involved the following changes. First, he attacked the perception of what God said. Second, he altered the definitions of words. Third, he played on her vanity by insisting that God was trying to prevent her from attaining her fullest potential. In other words, God was scared of her innate freedom.

Change agents today do the same things as they seek to pull people away from truth. First, they attack the perception of what God's Word says. They constantly go back to the Restoration Movement and catalog any instance they can use to chip away at our heritage. If they believed or practiced something in the Restoration, then why don't we?

Second, change agents alter the definition of words. A Christian becomes just a person who is sincerely following Christ rather than what Scripture prescribes as a believer immersed for the remission of sins who is being obedient to Christ.

Baptism is altered until it is a shell of its scriptural definition. Church becomes much more expansive than what Christ began and salvation becomes much less than what Jesus desired.

Third, change agents play on the vanity of man to expand the borders of fellowship in the church. They belittle brethren for being narrow minded, selfish, exclusive, snobby, and legalistic for seeking to be in the sanctified

Church of Christ. Derisive laughter meets those who attempt to maintain the fellowship God desires. By playing on people's emotions and guilt, they hope to shame people into submission. Change agents must reorient people to a new reality where all the rules have changed. They are savvy enough to know that these changes will be painful and provoke opposition. Therefore, they are very patient in their efforts. That which is bearing fruit today was sown many years ago. Those who are evaluating their proposals need to see the dangers of their poison fruit.

So with that said, now I hope you can see that there is a desperate need to expose the AD 70 change agents for what they are—first cousins to the "snake" of the Garden of Eden. Like Satan, they express that God said they would "not surely die" (Genesis 3:4).[4]

(NOTE: I have used several sermons, debates, and essays published by other men. I make no apology. It was necessary due to the lack of knowledge that I possessed at the beginning of this exercise. I wanted to cover as many topics as possible so there is some overlap between articles. I now understand this heresy that is currently gaining steam among the Lord's church. It must be stopped. The eldership of the local assemblies of the Lord's church must keep men such as teach this heresy out of our pulpits. It is hard to believe that mature Christian men that have once believed can fall so low as to believe the teaching of the AD 70 doctrine. I pray for their souls!)

Hebrews 10:26-27, 31
"For if we sin wilfully after that we have received the knowledge of the truth, there remaineth no more a sacrifice for sins, 27 but a certain fearful expectation of judgment, and a fierceness of fire which shall devour the adversaries...(verse 31) It is a fearful thing to fall into the hands of the living God."

---

[4] Richard Mansel, managing editor, http://www.forthright.net/editorial/lend_a_hand.html, http://www.forthright.net, Forthright Magazine, May 14, 2009 Edition

Realized Eschatology

We will begin our study of the teaching of A.D. 70 Doctrine by explaining their doctrine, what they believe and teach: So let's get started...

In *The Parousia* written by James Stuart Russell, page vi says, "The arguments here have convinced many that Christ's second advent actually took place in the first century of the Christian era. Russell took much joy each time another person adopted this view."

The word "Parousia" (par-oo-see-ah) is not a household word, but students of end time prophecy know it is a reference to the *Second Coming of Christ*. Russell believed the 2nd coming occurred in the first century at the destruction of Jerusalem in AD 70, his view is labeled "Preterist."

The word "Preterist" is another prophetic term with which many are unfamiliar. According to Webster's Unabridged Dictionary, a Preterist is "a theologian who believes the prophecies of the apocalypse have already been fulfilled." A preterist is the opposite of a futurist. Futurists teach that the three major endtime events (2nd coming of Christ, resurrection, judgment) are still future in fulfillment, whereas preterists teach these events have already been fulfilled.

Some wonder what difference does it make? Everything crucial to Christianity is at risk. The Deity of Christ, the integrity of the apostles and prophets, worship, and the inspiration of the New Testament is at stake.

CHAPTER 1
Reviewing the Parousia

Summary and Conclusion of Russell's The Parousia [5]

I guess it is a little strange to begin with the conclusion of The Parousia. In this case, the conclusion summarizes his teaching without going through a book of nearly 600 pages.

We have now reached a point in our investigation where it is possible to take a complete and connected survey of the whole field which we have

---

[5] The Parousia, James Stuart Russell, pp 531-554

traversed, and to observe the unity and consistency of the prophetic system developed in the New Testament. This then is the conclusion drawn by Mr. Russell in his famous book The Parousia. The following comments by Mr. Russell are taken verbatim as he wrote them starting on page 531 of his book. The book is such a rambling of mis-mash that I didn't see the need to expose you to all of the ends and outs of his theology of this subject. Therefore, I leave it for each of you to read his book or go to the internet and read it online.

Now we can get started:

1. We find that the Gospel dispensation does not come upon us as an independent and isolated scheme—a new beginning in the divine government of the world—but that it *implies and assumes* the relation of God to Israel in past ages. The whole philosophy of Jewish history is condensed into a single phrase, 'the kingdom of God;' and it is this kingdom which, first John the Baptist, as the herald of the coming king, and next the King Himself, the Lord Jesus Christ, proclaimed as being 'at hand.' *(This is true but the "kingdom of God" in these passages refers to the church that is coming—not Jesus himself).*

2. We find that John the Baptist adopts the warnings of Old Testament prophecy, especially of the last of the prophets, Malachi, and predicts that the coming of the kingdom would be the coming of wrath upon Israel. He declares that 'the axe is already laid to the root of the tree;' his cry is, 'Flee from the coming wrath,' plainly intimating that a time of judgment was fast approaching.

3. Our Lord affirms the same speedy coming of judgment upon the land and people of Israel; and He further connects this judgment with His own coming in glory,—the Parousia. This event stands forth most prominently in the New Testament; to this every eye is directed, to this every inspired messenger points. It is represented as the nucleus and centre of a cluster of great events; the end of the age, or close of the Jewish economy; the destruction of the city and temple of Jerusalem; the judgment of the guilty nation; the resurrection of the dead; the reward of the faithful; the consummation of the kingdom of God. All these transactions are declared to be coincident with the Parousia.

4. It is demonstrable by the express testimony of our Lord, the uniform and concurrent teaching of His apostles, and the universal expectation of the church of the apostolic age *that the Parousia and its accompanying events were represented as nigh at hand;* and not only so, but as about to happen within the limits of a given period; that is to say, in the time of the apostles and their contemporaries, so that many or most of them might expect to witness the great consummation. This is the main point of the whole question and must be decided by the authority of the Scriptures themselves. While the proof ought to be rigorously demanded and the evidence thoroughly sifted, it ought also to be dispassionately considered without resorting to non natural interpretation, uncritical and unfair evasion, or violent wresting of the plain sense of words.

5. Without going over the ground already traversed, it may suffice here to appeal to three distinct and decisive declarations of our Lord respecting the time of His coming, each of them accompanied with a solemn affirmation:—

> (1) 'Verily I say unto you, Ye shall not have gone over the cities of Israel, till the Son of man be come' (Matt. 10:23).
>
> (2) 'Verily I say unto you, there be some standing here, which shall not taste of death, till they see the Son of man coming in his kingdom' (Matt. 16:28).
>
> (3) 'Verily I say unto you, This generation shall not pass, till all these things be fulfilled' (Matt. 24:34).

The plain grammatical meaning of these statements will be fully discussed in these pages. No violence can extort from them any other sense than the obvious and unambiguous one, viz. that our Lord's second coming would take place within the limits of the existing generation.

6. The doctrine of the apostles with regard to the coming of the Lord is in perfect harmony with this. Nothing can be more evident than that they all believed and taught the speedy return of the Lord. From the first speech of Peter on the day of Pentecost to the last utterance of John in the Apocalypse, this conviction is clearly and constantly expressed. To say that the apostles were themselves ignorant of the time of their Lord's re-

turn, and therefore could have no belief on the subject,—could not teach what they did not know,—is to contradict their own express and reiterated assertions. True, they did not know, and did not teach, 'that day and that hour;' they did not say that He would come in a particular month of a particular year, but they assuredly did give the churches to understand that He was coming quickly; that they might soon expect to see Him; and they never ceased to exhort them to maintain the attitude of constant watchfulness and preparation.

It is not necessary to do more than advert to some of the leading testimonies borne by the apostles to the speedy coming of the Lord:—

(1) St. Paul gives great prominence in his epistles to this cherished hope of the church.

> **a.** In the First Epistle to the Thessalonians he implies the possibility of the Lord's coming in his and their lifetime,— 'We which are alive and remain unto the coming of the Lord.' He also prays that 'their spirit, soul, and body may be preserved blameless unto the coming of our Lord Jesus Christ.'
>
> **b.** In the Second Epistle to the Thessalonians (which is often erroneously understood to teach that the coming of Christ was not at hand, but which teaches precisely the contrary doctrine) he comforts the suffering believers with the promise that they would obtain rest from their present sufferings 'when the Lord Jesus was revealed from heaven,' etc. (2 Thess. 1:7).
>
> **c.** In the First Epistle to the Corinthians the apostle speaks of believers as 'waiting for the coming of the Lord Jesus Christ.' He warns them that 'the time is short;' that 'the end of the age,' or 'ends of the ages,' are come upon them; that 'the Lord is at hand.'
>
> **d.** In the Second Epistle to the Corinthians St. Paul expresses his confidence that though he might die before the coming of the Lord, yet God would raise him from the dead, and present him along with those who survived to that period.
>
> **e.** In the Epistle to the Romans St. Paul speaks of 'the glory about to be revealed;' of the whole creation waiting for the manifestation of the Son of God; of salvation being near, 'nearer than

when they first believed;' that 'it is now high time to awake out of sleep;' that 'the night is far spent, and the day at hand;' that 'God will bruise Satan under their feet shortly.'

f. In the Epistles to the Ephesians, Philippians, and Colossians the apostle speaks of 'the day of Christ' as the period of hope, perfection, and glory to which they were looking forward, and he declares emphatically, 'The Lord is at hand.'

g. In like manner, in the Epistles to Timothy and Titus the expectation of the Parousia is conspicuous. Timothy is exhorted to keep the commandment inviolate 'until the appearing of our Lord Jesus Christ.' 'He is about to judge the living and the dead at his appearing, and his kingdom.' Christians are exhorted to be looking 'for that blessed hope, even the glorious appearing of the great God and our Saviour, Jesus Christ.'

(2) St. James represents the coming of the Lord as just at hand. 'The last days' are come. Suffering Christians are exhorted to 'be patient unto the coming of the Lord.' They are assured that 'it is drawing nigh;' that the Judge standeth before the door.'

(3) St. Peter, like St. Paul, gives great prominence to the Parousia and its related events.

a. On the day of Pentecost he declared that those were 'the last days' predicted by the prophet Joel, introductory to 'the great and terrible day of the Lord.'

b. In his First Epistle he affirms that it was 'the last time;' that God was 'ready to judge the living and the dead;' 'that the end of all things was at hand;' that 'the time had come when judgment was to begin at the house of God.'

c. In his Second Epistle he exhorts Christians to be 'looking for and hasting unto the coming of the day of God;' and depicts the approaching dissolution of 'heaven and earth.'

(4) The Epistle to the Hebrews speaks of 'the last days' as now present; it is 'the end of the age;' the day is seen to be 'approaching;' 'Yet a little, little while, and he that is coming will come, and will not tarry.'

(5) St. John confirms and completes the testimony of his fellow-apostles; it is 'the last time;' 'antichrist has come;' 'he is already in the world.' Christians are exhorted so to live that they may not be ashamed before Christ at His coming.

Finally, the Apocalypse is full of the Parousia: 'Behold, he cometh with clouds;' 'The time is at hand;' 'Behold, I come quickly.'

Such is a rapid sketch of the apostolic testimony to the speedy coming of the Lord. It would have been strange if, with such assurances and such exhortations, the apostolic churches had not lived in constant and eager expectation of the Parousia. That they did so we have the clearest evidence in the New Testament, and we can conceive the mighty influence which this faith and hope must have had upon Christian life and character.

But, admitting, what cannot well be denied, that the apostles and early Christians did cherish these expectations, and that their belief was founded on the teaching of our Lord, the question arises, Were they not mistaken in their expectation? This is practically to ask, Were the apostles permitted to fall into error themselves, and to lead others into a like delusion, with respect to a matter of fact which they had abundant opportunities of knowing; which must frequently have been the subject of conversation and conference among themselves; which they never failed to keep before the attention of the churches, and about which they were all agreed?

There are critics who do not scruple to affirm that the apostles were mistaken, and that time has proved the fallacy of their anticipations. They tell us that either they misunderstood the teaching of their Master, or that He too was under an erroneous impression. This is of course to set aside the claims of the apostles to speak authoritatively as the inspired messengers of Christ, and to undermine the very foundations of the Christian faith.

There are others, more reverential in their treatment of Scripture, who acknowledge that the apostles were indeed mistaken, but that this mistake was, for wise reasons, permitted,—that, in fact, the error was highly beneficial in its results: it stimulated hope, it fortified courage, it inspired devotion." *

(* 'For ages the world's hope has been the second advent. The early church expected it in their own day,—"We which are alive and remain unto the coming of the Lord." The Saviour Himself had said, "This generation shall not pass till all these things be fulfilled." Yet the Son of man has never come. In the first centuries the early Christians believed that the millennial advent was close; they heard the warning of the apostle, brief and sharp, "The time is short." Now, suppose that instead of this they had seen all the dreary page of church history unrolled; suppose that they had known that after two thousand years the world would have scarcely spelled out three letters of the meaning of Christianity, where would have been those gigantic efforts, that life spent as on the very brink of eternity, which characterize the days of the early church?—F. W. Robertson, Sermon on the Illusiveness of Life.)

'If the Christians of the first centuries,' says Hengstenberg, 'had foreseen that the second coming of Christ would not take place for eighteen hundred years, how much weaker an impression would this doctrine have made upon them than when they were expecting Him every hour, and were told to watch because He would come like a thief in the night, at an hour when they looked not for Him!' (Hengstenberg, Christology, vol. iv. p. 443.)

But neither can this explanation be accepted as satisfactory. Unquestionably the first Christians did receive an immense impulse to their courage and zeal from their firm belief in the speedy advent of the Lord; but was this a hope that after all made them ashamed? Must we conclude that the indomitable courage and devotion of a Paul rested mainly on a delusion? Were the martyrs and confessors of the primitive age only mistaken enthusiasts? We confess that such a conclusion is revolting to all our conceptions of Christianity as a revelation of divine truth by the instrumentality of inspired men. If the apostles misunderstood or misrepresented the teaching of Christ in regard to a matter of fact, respecting which they had the most ample opportunities of information, what dependence can be placed upon their testimony as to matters of faith, where the liability to error is so much greater? Such explanations are fitted to unsettle the foundations of confidence in apostolic teaching; and it is not easy to see how they are compatible with any practical belief in inspiration.

There is *another theory*, however, by which *many suppose* that the credit of the apostles is saved, and yet room left for avoiding the acceptance of their apparent teaching on the subject of the coming of Christ. This is, by the hypothesis of a primary and partial fulfillment of their predictions in their own time, to be followed and completed by an ultimate and plenary fulfillment at the end of human history. According to this view, the anticipations of the apostles were not wholly erroneous. Something really did take place that might be called 'a coming of the Lord,' 'a judgment day.' Their predictions received a quasi fulfillment in the destruction of Jerusalem and in the judgment of the guilty nation. That consummation at the close of the Jewish age was a type of another and infinitely greater catastrophe, when the whole human race will be brought before the judgment seat of Christ and the earth consumed by a general conflagration. This is probably the view which is most commonly accepted by the majority of expositors and readers of the New Testament at the present day. The first objection to this hypothesis is that it has no foundation in the teaching of the Scriptures. There is not a scintilla of evidence that the apostles and primitive Christians had any suspicion of a twofold reference in the predictions of Jesus concerning the end. No hint is anywhere dropped that a primary and partial fulfillment of His sayings was to take place in that generation, but that the complete and exhaustive fulfillment was reserved for a future and far distant period. The very contrary is the fact. What can be more comprehensive and conclusive than our Lord's words, 'Verily I say unto you, This generation shall not pass, till ALL these things be fulfilled'? What critical torture has been applied to these words to extort from them some other meaning than their obvious and natural one! How has yeveà been hunted through all its lineage and genealogy to discover that it may not mean the persons then living on the earth! But all such efforts are wholly futile. While the words remain in the text, their plain and obvious sense will prevail over all the glosses and perversions of ingenious criticism. The hypothesis of a twofold fulfillment receives no countenance from the Scriptures. We have only to read the language in which the apostles speak of the approaching consummation to be convinced that they had one, and only one, great event in view, and that they thought and spoke of it as just at hand.

This brings us to another objection to the hypothesis of a double, or even manifold, fulfillment of the predictions in the New Testament, viz. that it proceeds from a fundamentally erroneous conception of the real significance and grandeur or that great crisis in the divine government of the world which is marked by the Parousia. There are not a few who seem to think that if our Lord's prophecy on the Mount of Olives, and the predictions of the apostles of the coming of Christ in glory, meant no more than the destruction of Jerusalem, and were fulfilled in that event, then all their announcements and expectations ended in a mere fiasco, and the historical reality answers very feebly and inadequately to the magnificent prophecy. There is reason to believe that the true significance and grandeur of that great event are very little appreciated by many. The destruction of Jerusalem was not a mere thrilling incident in the drama of history, like the siege of Troy or the downfall of Carthage, closing a chapter in the annals of a state or a people. It was an event which has no parallel in history. It was the outward and visible sign of a great epoch in the divine government of the world. It was the close of one dispensation and the commencement of another. It marked the inauguration of a new order of things. The Mosaic economy,—which had been ushered in by the miracles of Egypt, the lightnings and thunderings of Sinai, and the glorious manifestations of Jehovah to Israel,—after subsisting for more than fifteen centuries, was now abolished. The peculiar relation between the Most High and the covenant nation was dissolved. The Messianic kingdom, that is, the administration of the divine government by the Mediator, so far, at least, as Israel was concerned, reached its culminating point. The kingdom so long predicted, hoped for, prayed for, was now fully come. The final act of the King was to sit upon the throne of His glory and judge His people. He could then 'deliver up the kingdom to God, even the Father.' This is the significance of the destruction of Jerusalem according to the showing of the Word of God. It was not an isolated fact, a solitary catastrophe,—it was the centre of a group of related and coincident events, not only in the material, but in the spiritual world; not only on earth, but in heaven and in hell; some of them being cognizable by the senses and capable of historical confirmation, and others not.

Perhaps it may be said that such an explanation of the predictions of the New Testament, instead of relieving the difficulty, embarrasses and perplexes us more than ever. It is possible to believe in the fulfillment of predictions which take effect in the visible and outward order of things, because we have historical evidence of that fulfillment; but how can we be expected to believe in fulfillments which are said to have taken place in the region of the spiritual and invisible when we have no witnesses to depose to the facts? We can implicitly believe in the accomplishment of all that was predicted respecting the horrors of the siege of Jerusalem, the burning of the temple, and the demolition of the city, because we have the testimony of Josephus to the facts; but how can we believe in a coming of the Son of man, in a resurrection of the dead, in an act of judgment ,when we have nothing but the word of prophecy to rely upon, and no Josephus to vouch for the historical accuracy of the facts?

The A.D. 70 Theory

To this it can only be said in reply that the demand for human testimony to events in the region of the unseen is not altogether reasonable. If we receive them at all, it must be on the word of Him Who declared that all these things would assuredly take place before that generation passed away. But, after all, is the demand upon our faith in this matter so very excessive? A large portion of these predictions we know to have been literally and punctually fulfilled; we recognize in that accomplishment a remarkable proof of the truth of the Word of God and the superhuman prescience that foresaw and foretold the future. Could anything have been less probable at the time when our Lord delivered His prophetic discourse than the total destruction of the temple, the razing of the city, and the ruin of the nation in the lifetime of the existing generation? What can be more minute and particular than the signs of the end enumerated by our Lord? What can be more precise and literal than the fulfillment of them?

But the part which confessedly has been fulfilled, and which is vouched for by uninspired history, is inseparably bound up with another portion which is not so vouched for. Nothing but a violent disruption can detach the one part of this prophecy from the other. It is one from beginning to end—a complete whole. The finest instrument cannot draw a line separating one portion which relates to that generation from another portion which relates to a different and distant period. Every part of it rests on the same foundation, and the whole is so linked and concatenated that all must stand or fall together. We are justified, therefore, in holding that the exact accomplishment of so much of the prophecy as comes within the cognizance of the senses, and is capable of being vouched for by human testimony, is a presumption and guarantee in favour of the exact fulfillment of that portion which lies within the region of the invisible and spiritual, and which cannot, in the nature of things, be attested by human evidence. This is not credulity, but reasonable faith, such as men fearlessly exercise in all their worldly transactions.

We conclude, therefore, that all the parts of our Lord's prediction refer to the same period and the same event; that the whole prophecy is one and indivisible, resting upon the same foundation of divine authority. Further, that all that was cognizable by the human senses is proved to have been fulfilled, and, therefore, we are not only warranted, but bound to assume the fulfillment of the remainder as not only credible, but certain.

As the result of the investigation we are landed in this dilemma: either the whole group of predictions, comprehending the destruction of Jerusalem, the coming of the Lord, the resurrection of the dead, and the rewarding of the faithful did take place before the passing away of that generation, as predicted by Christ, taught by the apostles, and expected by the whole church; or, else, the hope of the church was a delusion, the teaching of the apostles an error, the predictions of Jesus a dream.

There is no other alternative consistent with the fair grammatical interpretation of the words of Scripture. We may not tear the prophecy of Christ asunder and arbitrarily decide this is past, and that is future; this is fulfilled, and that unfulfilled. There is no pretext for such a division in the record of that discourse; like the seamless robe worn by Him who uttered it, it is all of one piece, 'woven from the top throughout.' The grammatical structure and the historical occasion alike imply the unity of the whole prophecy. Neither is there any 'verifying faculty' by which it is possible to distinguish between one part and another as belonging to different periods and epochs. Every attempt to draw such lines of distinction has proved a complete failure. The prophecy refuses to be so manipulated, and asserts its unity and homogeneity in spite of critical artifice or violence. We are compelled, therefore, by all these considerations, and chiefly by regard for the authority of Him whose word cannot be broken, to conclude that the Parousia, or second coming of Christ, with its connected and concomitant events, did take place, according to the Saviour's own prediction, at the period when Jerusalem was destroyed, and before the passing away of 'that generation.'

Here we might pause, for Scripture prophecy guides us no further. But the close of the æon is not the end of the world, and the fate of Israel teaches us nothing respecting the destiny of the human race. Whether we will or no, we cannot help speculating about the future and forecasting the ultimate fortunes of a world which has been the scene of such stupendous displays of divine judgment and mercy. It will probably be felt by some to be an unwelcome conclusion that the Apocalypse is not that syllabus of civil and ecclesiastical history which a mistaken theory of interpretation supposed it to be. It will seem to them that the extinction of those false lights, which they took for guiding stars, leaves them in total darkness about the future; and they will ask in perplexity, *Whither are we tending*? What is to be the end and consummation of human history? Is this earth, with its precious freight of immortal and eternal interests, advancing towards light and truth or hurrying into regions of darkness and distance from God?

Where nothing has been revealed it would be the height of presumption to prognosticate the future. 'It is not for us to know the times and the seasons which the Father hath put in his own power.' It has been said that 'the uninspired prophet is a fool,' and many instances approve the saying. Yet thus much it may be permitted us to conclude: there is no reason to despair about the future. There are some who tell us that as Judaism was a failure, so Christianity will be a failure also. We are not persuaded of this; we regard it rather as an impeachment of the divine wisdom and goodness. Judaism was never constituted to be a universal religion; it was essentially limited and national in its operation; but Christianity is made for man, and has proved its adaptation to every variety of the human family. It is indeed too true that the progress of Christianity in the world has been lamentably slow; and that, after eighteen centuries, it has not succeeded in banishing evil from the world, nor even from the regions where its influence has been most powerfully felt. Yet, after every allowance for its shortcomings, it still remains the mightiest moral force ever called into operation for purifying and ennobling the character of men. It is Christianity that differentiates the new world from the old; the modern from the ancient civilization. This is the new factor in human society and history which may claim the largest share in the beneficent reformations of the past and to which we may look for still greater results in the future. The philosophic historian recognizes in Christianity a new power, which 'from its very origin, and still more in its progress, entirely renovated the face of the world.' (Schlegel, Philosophy of History, Lect. x.)

Nor is there any symptom of decrepitude or exhaustion in the religion of Jesus after all the ages and conflicts, and revolutions of opinion through which it has come. It has stood the brunt of the most malignant persecution, and come off victorious. It has endured the ordeal of the most searching and hostile criticism, and come out of the fire unscathed. It has survived the more perilous patronage of pretended friends who have corrupted it into a superstition, perverted it into a policy, or degraded it into a trade. While the enemies of the Gospel predict its speedy extinction, it enters on a new career of conflict and victory. There is a perpetual tendency in Christianity to renew her youth, to regain the ideal of her pristine purity, and defecate herself from the impurities and accretions which are foreign to her nature. Never since the apostolic age were there greater vitality and vigour in the religion of the Cross than today. This is the age of Christian missions; and while all the other religions of the world have ceased to proselytize, and therefore to grow, Christianity goes forth to every land and nation, with the Bible in her hand and the proclamation of the glad tidings in her mouth, 'Believe in the Lord Jesus Christ and thou shalt be saved.'

The true interpretation of New Testament prophecy, instead of leaving us in darkness, encourages hope. It relieves the gloom which hung over a world which was believed to be destined to perish. There is no reason to infer that because Jerusalem was destroyed the world must burn; or, because the apostate nation was condemned, the human race must be consigned to perdition. All this sinister anticipation rests upon an erroneous interpretation of Scripture; and, the fallacies being cleared away, the prospect brightens with a glorious hope. We may trust the God of Love. He has not forsaken the earth, and He governs the world on a plan which He has not indeed disclosed to us, but which we may be well assured will finally evolve the highest good of the creature and the brightest glory of the Creator.

It may, indeed, seem strange and unaccountable that we should now be left without any of those divine manifestations and revelations which in other ages God was pleased to vouchsafe to men. We seem in some respects farther off from heaven than those ages were when voices and visions reminded men of the nearness of the Unseen. We may say, with the Jews of the captivity, 'We see not our signs: there is no more any prophet: neither is there among us any that knoweth how long,' Ps. 74:9).

Two thousand nine years (updated mgb) have rolled away since a voice was heard upon earth saying, 'Thus saith the Lord.' It is as if a door had been shut in heaven and the direct intercourse of God with man were cut off; and we seem at a disadvantage as compared with those who were favoured with 'visions and revelations of the Lord.' Yet, even in this we may not judge correctly. Doubtless it is better as it is. The presence of the Holy Spirit with the disciples was declared by our Lord to be more than a compensation for His own absence. That Spirit dwells with us, and in us, and it is His office 'to take of Christ's, and to shew it unto us.' We have also the written Word of God, and in this we enjoy an incalculable superiority over the former days. Better the written Word than the living prophet. But should it be needful for the welfare and guidance of mankind that God should again manifest Himself, there is no presumption against further revelations. Why should it be thought that God has spoken His last word to men? But it is for Him to choose, and not for us to dictate. It may well be that even now, in ways unsuspected by us, He is speaking to man. 'God fulfils himself in many ways, and human history is as full of God today as in the ages of miracle and prophecy. Far from us be that incredulity which despairs of Christianity and of man. Surely, it was not in vain that Jesus said, 'I am the Light of the World.' 'God sent not his Son into the world to condemn the world, but that the world might be saved.' 'I, if I be lifted up from the earth, will draw all men unto myself.'

That favoured apostle who more than any other seems to have comprehended 'the breadth, and length, and depth, and height of the love of Christ,' suggests to us ideas of the extent and efficiency of the great redemption which our latent incredulity can scarcely receive. He does not hesitate to affirm that the restorative work of Christ will ultimately more than repair the ruin wrought by sin. 'As by one man's disobedience the many were made sinners, so by the obedience of One shall the many be made righteous.' There would be no point in this comparison if 'the many' on the one side of the equation bore no proportion to 'the many' on the other side. But this is not all: the redemptive work of Christ does more than redress the balance: it outweighs, and that immeasurably, the counterpoise of evil. 'Where sin abounded, grace did beyond measure abound: that as sin reigned in death, even so might grace reign in righteousness unto eternal life through Jesus Christ our Lord' (Rom. 5:19-21).

It does not fall within the scope of this discussion to argue on philosophical grounds the natural probability of a reign of truth and righteousness on the earth; we are happy to be assured of the consummation on higher and safer grounds, even the promises of Him who has taught us to pray, 'Thy will be done in earth, as it is done in heaven.' For every God-taught prayer contains a prophecy, and conveys a promise. This world belongs no more to the devil, but to God. Christ has redeemed it, and will recover it, and draw all men unto Him.

Now let's take a look at what *Mr. Wayne Petty* of Athens, Alabama, is teaching about this A.D. 70 Doctrine. He left the Lord's Body where we were worshipping together. He was an elder when he resigned and left our assembly. While worshipping with Wayne, I always had the highest regard for his abilities to teach the Bible. We were in many Bible classes together over about (4) years until he left in 2003. He further informed me that he has been studying this teaching of Dawson, Russell, and King since 2005. I never did hear him speak on this subject and did not know that he held this view until a few years ago. He put the following article on the website of Sam Dawson. It is presented verbatim as he gave it to me to use for this paper. www.gospelthemes.com/e-petty-pretintro.htm

CHAPTER 2

The Second Coming of Christ, the Resurrection, and the Judgment --Their Timing and Nature
A Brief Introduction

The Return of Christ, the Resurrection, and the Judgment are all connected in prophecy and fulfilled at the destruction of Jerusalem. This brief study succinctly reveals the truth on the "Big Three" of eschatology.

Since we are saved by God's grace through faith, our salvation does not depend on a perfect understanding of every Bible subject--thankfully. But at the same time, we seek to grow in our knowledge of what has been revealed to us through the Bible.

As disciples, it is our task to continue to study God's word and to seek a greater understanding of what He has revealed. Sometimes we may find we have to change our minds about fundamental concepts. This, of course, is very difficult to do. But if we are committed to the search for truth, we will be willing to review any conviction. With this in mind, please consider the following.

The majority of believers in Christ today view the Second Coming, the Resurrection, and the Judgment as events that yet lie in the future. One of the main reasons for this conviction is that the Biblical account is full of seemingly literal descriptions that are linked to these events.

Note the following for example:

> "...the Son of Man *coming on the clouds*..." (Mt. 24.30),
>
> "...the trumpet will sound, and *the dead will be raised* incorruptible" (1 Cor. 15.52), and
>
> "...the dead, small and great, *standing before God, and books were opened*...and the dead *were judged* according to their works..." (Rev. 20.12).

So it is reasoned that if the *nature* of these events is literal, then the *time* of their fulfillment is obviously in the future.

This paper takes the opposite approach. *We will show that Scripture indicates that the time of Jesus' Coming, the Resurrection, and the Judgment was confined to the first century.* If this is true, then we will have reason to reevaluate the literal-sounding images to see if they actually may be prophetic or figurative descriptions of events that are spiritual in their nature.

The Time of Their Fulfillment

We will now consider what the Bible teaches regarding the time of the fulfillment of the Second Coming, the Resurrection, and the Judgment. *We will find that the three events are concurrent and the time of their fulfillment can be established exclusively from Jesus' own teaching and His application of Daniel, the prophet.*

The Time of His Coming and the Judgment

In that Generation

Jesus foretold his coming in judgment to his apostles:

> "For the Son of Man *will come* [is about to come--YLT] in the glory of His Father with His angels, and then He *will reward*

each according to his works. Assuredly, I say to you, there are some standing here who shall not taste death till they see the Son of Man coming in His kingdom." (Mt. 16.27-28) [YLT--Young's Literal Translation]

Notice that Jesus here declares that His coming, in judgment ("to reward each"), was "about to come" and would be within the lifetime of some of those present.

At the "End of the Age"

Previously, in the Parable of the Wheat and the Tares (Weeds), Jesus taught some Jewish disciples that *His coming, in judgment* would be at the *"end of the age."*

> Another parable He put forth to them, saying: "The kingdom of heaven is like a man who sowed good seed in his field; but while men slept, his enemy came and sowed tares among the wheat and went his way. But when the grain had sprouted and produced a crop, then the tares also appeared. So the servants of the owner came and said to him, 'Sir, did you not sow good seed in your field? How then does it have tares?' He said to them, 'An enemy has done this.' The servants said to him, 'Do you want us then to go and gather them up?' But he said, 'No, lest while you gather up the tares you also uproot the wheat with them. Let both grow together until the harvest, and at the time of harvest I will say to the reapers, *"First gather together the tares and bind them in bundles to burn them, but gather the wheat into my barn."'"* [judgment--WP]

> Then Jesus sent the multitude away and went into the house. And His disciples came to Him, saying, "Explain to us the parable of the tares of the field." He answered and said to them: "He who sows the good seed is the Son of Man. The field is the world, the good seeds are the sons of the kingdom, but the tares are the sons of the wicked one. The enemy who sowed them is the devil, *the harvest is the end of the age,* and the reapers are the angels. Therefore as the tares are gathered and burned in the fire, so it will be at *the end of this age.* The Son of Man *will send out His angels* [at his "coming"--WP], and they will gather out of His kingdom all things that offend, and those who practice lawlessness, and will cast them into the furnace of fire. There will be wailing

and gnashing of teeth. Then the righteous will shine forth as the sun in the kingdom of their Father. He who has ears to hear, let him hear! (Mt. 13.24-30; 36-43)

When Jesus said this, the "Christian Age" had not yet begun. "This age" (v. 40) for Jesus at that time was the Mosaic Age:

> But when the fullness of the time had come, God sent forth His Son, born of a woman, *born under the law,* to redeem those who were under the law, that we might receive the adoption as sons. (Gal. 4.4-5)

[The Greek word translated "age" in this context (and others below) is incorrectly rendered "world" in some translations. The original word, *aion*, describes a period of time; not a planet.]

So, Jesus' coming, in judgment, would be within the lifetime of some of the apostles--at the "end of the (Mosaic) age."

During the "Time of the End"

Further, at the end of the Parable of the Wheat and Tares, in Mt. 13.43, Jesus quotes from Dan. 12.3. In this way, Jesus shows the events of the parable to be the fulfillment of Dan. 12. When we look at the rest of Dan. 12, we find out more about when the "end of the age" would take place.

Jesus placed "the end of the age" during "the time of the end" as revealed to Daniel:

> "But you, Daniel, shut up the words, and seal the book until *the time of the end;* many shall run to and fro, and knowledge shall increase." (Dan. 12.4)

It would be when the power of the holy people (the Old Covenant Jews, Daniel 9:15-20) would be "completely shattered":

> Then I, Daniel, looked; and there stood two others, one on this riverbank and the other on that riverbank. And one said to the man clothed in linen, who was above the waters of the river, "How long shall the fulfillment of these wonders be?" Then I heard the man clothed in linen, who was above the waters of the river, when he held up his right hand and his left hand to heaven, and swore by Him who lives forever, that it shall be for a time,

times, and half a time; and *when the power of the holy people has been completely shattered, all these things shall be finished.* (Dan. 12.5-7)

In the wider context, we find that the power of the holy people would be completely shattered when Jerusalem and the temple would be destroyed:

"And after the sixty-two weeks Messiah shall be cut off, but not for Himself; And the people of the prince who is to come *Shall destroy the city* [Jerusalem, Dan. 9.16--WP] *and the sanctuary* [the temple--WP]. The end of it shall be with a flood, And till the end of the war desolations are determined. Then he shall confirm a covenant with many for one week; But in the middle of the week He shall bring an end to sacrifice and offering. And on the wing of abominations shall be one who makes desolate, Even until *the consummation* which is determined, Is poured out on the desolate." (Dan. 9.26-27)

"The end of the (Mosaic) age" would take place when the "power of the holy people" would be "completely shattered"--when Jerusalem and the temple would be destroyed.

Jesus' Return at the Destruction of the Temple

The foregoing analysis of the "end of the age" coincides perfectly with what Jesus described to the apostles on the Mount of Olives (Mt. 24-25). The disciples had already heard the teaching of Jesus that we have just noticed (Mt. 16, Mt. 13). And, as faithful Jews, they would have been familiar with the prophecies of Daniel. So, it follows that after hearing Jesus predict the destruction of the temple, they asked the natural questions-- "when" would this happen and "what" would be the sign of His coming-- which would be at the "end of the age":

Then Jesus went out and departed from the temple, and His disciples came up to show Him the buildings of *the temple.* And Jesus said to them, "Do you not see all these things? Assuredly, I say to you, *not one stone shall be left here upon another, that shall not be thrown down."* Now as He sat on the Mount of Olives, the disciples came to Him privately, saying, "Tell us, when will these things be? And what will be the sign of Your coming, and of *the end of the age?"* (Mt. 24.1-3).

A survey of Jesus' answer (Mt. 24-25) reveals the same items that we have already noticed:

1. Destruction of the temple (24.2)

2. His coming (24.2; 25.31)

3. In judgment (24.2; 25.32ff)

4. Jesus mentions Daniel by name and alludes to Dan. 9.27 commenting on the "abomination of desolation" at "the end" (the "end of the age") (24.13-15)

5. On clouds (24.30)

6. With glory (24.30, 36; 25.31)

7. With angels (25.31)

8. The gathering of the elect (24.31)

9. His coming would be within the generation then living (24.34)

10. After judgment, some to "everlasting punishment," some to "eternal life" (25.46)

Thus, from these few passages, we conclude that the Coming of Christ and the Judgment would take place in that generation--within the lifetime of some of the apostles (Mt. 16, 24, 25), at the end of the Mosaic Age (Mt. 13). This would be when the "power of the holy people was completely shattered" (Dan. 12), at the destruction of the temple and Jerusalem (Dan. 9, Mt. 24).

The Time of the Resurrection

But there is more in Daniel 12--we find that the time of the judgment at the "end of the age" was also to be *the time of the resurrection!* In fact, the very verse from Daniel (12.3) that Jesus quoted in the Parable of the Wheat and Tares (Mt. 13.43) is a description of some of those who would be raised. Look at Dan. 12.2-3:

And many of *those who sleep in the dust of the earth shall awake,* Some to *everlasting life,* Some to shame and ever-

lasting contempt. Those who are wise shall shine Like the brightness of the firmament, And those who turn many to righteousness Like the stars forever and ever.

Clearly, "those who are wise that shine" are those who slept "in the dust of the earth" and would awake to "everlasting life." These are the same ones in the parable who are symbolized by the wheat that would be harvested at "the end of the age" and gathered into barns. Those who would awake from "the dust of the earth" to "everlasting contempt" would be the tares that would be burned at the "end of the age." *Here resurrection is inextricably linked to judgment.* They were to be raised so that they could be judged.

Further, Daniel himself was to be one of those who would sleep in the "dust of the earth" who would rise to "everlasting life." Daniel was told that he personally would rise at the "end of the age":

> "But you, go your way till the end; for you shall rest, and will arise to your inheritance at the end of the days [end of the age--NASB]." (Dan. 12.13)

So, we have now established, exclusively from Jesus' own teaching, that the Resurrection was to be at the same time as His Coming and the Judgment--all at "the end of the (Mosaic) age" (Mt. 16.27-28; Mt. 13; and Dan. 12).

Resurrection--A Promise to Ancient Israel

But how can this be? Most today see the resurrection as a promise to Christians at the end of the "Christian Age"!

Actually, the resurrection was primarily a promise to ancient Israel. In his defense before Herod Agrippa, Paul said that the resurrection was the hope of Israel, and that the twelve tribes hoped to attain it:

> And now I stand and am judged *for the hope of the promise made by God to our fathers.* To this promise *our twelve tribes,* earnestly serving God night and day, *hope to attain.* For this hope's sake, King Agrippa, I am accused by the Jews. *Why should it be thought incredible by you that God raises the dead?* (Ac. 26.6-8)

Previously, before Roman Procurator Festus, he said that the resurrection promise was written in the Law and the Prophets:

> But this I confess to you, that according to the Way which they call a sect, so I worship the God of my fathers, believing all things which are *written in the Law and in the Prophets.* I have hope in God, which they themselves also accept, that there will be [is about to be--YLT] *a resurrection of the dead,* both of the just and the unjust. This being so, I myself always strive to have a conscience without offense toward God and men. (Ac. 24.14-15).

Paul here alludes to the prophet Daniel. He believed what the prophet wrote about the resurrection of the just and the unjust (Dan. 12.2), and he believed it to be imminent.

This may seem foreign to us, but the Jews of the first century were familiar with this teaching. Jesus, in a discourse by the Sea of Galilee, taught the Jews that He was the "bread of life" and those who believed Him to be the Messiah would have "everlasting life" and He would raise them up at "the last day" (John 6.22ff).

Also, note the following conversation about the resurrection between Martha, a Jew, and Jesus on the occasion of her brother's death. Note that this discussion takes place well *before the "Christian Age" begins:*

> Now Martha, as soon as she heard that Jesus was coming, went and met Him, but Mary was sitting in the house. Now Martha said to Jesus, "Lord, if You had been here, my brother would not have died. But even now I know that whatever You ask of God, God will give You." Jesus said to her, "Your brother will rise again." Martha said to Him, *"I know that he will rise again in the resurrection at the last day."* (John 11.20-24)

Of course, we now know that Jesus was telling her that He was going to physically raise her brother, Lazarus, from the dead. But she does not seem to understand this. Consider her comment about a resurrection on "the last day." *She was describing the very concept we have just seen in Daniel 12 and in Jesus' teaching in John 6--resurrection at the "end of the age" (the Mosaic Age) on the "last day."* (We will have more comments on this text below.)

Paul: All Three Events Were Imminent

In conclusion of our discussion regarding the time of these events, look at one more passage in which all three are described as concurrent and imminent. In about AD 60, Paul tells Timothy that Jesus' *judgment* of "the dead" (i.e. those *resurrected*) was about to take place at Jesus' "appearing" (i.e. His *"coming"*):

> I charge you therefore before God and the Lord Jesus Christ, *who will judge [is about to judge--YLT] the living and the dead at His appearing* and His kingdom: Preach the word! Be ready in season and out of season. Convince, rebuke, exhort, with all longsuffering and teaching. (2 Tim. 4.1-2)

The Roman armies destroyed Jerusalem in AD 70. Not one stone of the temple was left upon another. Thus, we conclude that the Second Coming of Jesus, the Resurrection, and the Judgment all took place at that time-- the end of the Mosaic Age as predicted by Daniel and Jesus.

The Nature of the Second Coming, the Resurrection, and the Judgment

The correct understanding of the *timing* of these events leads us to a correct understanding of their *nature*.

We know these three events took place at that time because of Jesus' teaching. We also know they took place at that time because they were linked by scripture to an historical event--the destruction of Jerusalem.

Yet, where is the historical record of Jesus Christ travelling on an actual storm cloud? And where can we read of millions of dead people coming to life and exiting tomb and grave?

The Nature of His Coming and the Judgment

Did Jesus actually come "on a cloud"; and were the dead actually raised and judged? Yes, He did and, yes, they were--but perhaps what we thought were literal descriptions in scripture are not literal after all.

For example, Jesus describes Himself as "coming on the clouds":

> Then the sign of the Son of Man will appear in heaven, and then all the tribes of the earth will mourn, and they will see the Son of Man *coming on the clouds of heaven* with power and great glory. (Mt. 24.30)

In comparison, note that in the Old Testament, Jehovah is depicted as "coming on a cloud" in judgment against Egypt:

> The burden against Egypt. Behold, *the LORD rides on a swift cloud,* And will come into Egypt; The idols of Egypt will totter at His presence, And the heart of Egypt will melt in its midst. (Isa. 19.1)

Yet, the Father did not take some visible form and ride a cloud--the apostle John taught, "No one has seen God at any time." (John 1.18).

Rather, Jesus, a Jewish rabbi teaching other Jews, is using familiar imagery (that the Jews had heard before) regarding His own coming in judgment against Jerusalem. It is the same picture that Jehovah used of His coming in judgment against Egypt.

We see further similarity to other figurative Old Testament images. Compare what Jesus said describing His judgment against Jerusalem to what Jehovah said (through Isaiah) some 750 years earlier describing judgment against Babylon:

> "Immediately after the tribulation of those days *the sun will be darkened, and the moon will not give its light;* the stars will fall from heaven, and the powers of the heavens will be shaken." (Mt. 24.29)

> For the stars of heaven and their constellations Will not give their light; *The sun will be darkened* in its going forth, And *the moon will not cause its light to shine.* (Isa. 13.10)

Jesus' first century Jewish audience, being familiar with the prophets, would have immediately recognized the same figurative picture of judgment used in Isaiah. On the other hand, in modern times many of us lacking an adequate knowledge of the Old Testament have incorrectly concluded such a description to be literal.

Thus, we conclude that these images (and many others) figuratively illustrate the spiritual events of the Coming and the Judgment.

The Nature of the Resurrection

In regard to the resurrection, since history shows no record of widespread reanimation of deceased human bodies in AD 70, we reason that the "end-of-the-age" resurrection described by Daniel was also a "spiritual" event. Let's test this idea as we study Jesus' and Paul's teaching on the nature of the resurrection.

Jesus on the Nature of the Resurrection

Now we return to the John 11 passage noted above. After Martha answered with her understanding of "the resurrection on the last day," Jesus comments further:

> Jesus said to her, "I am the resurrection and the life. He who believes in Me, *though he may die, he shall live. And whoever lives and believes in Me shall never die.* Do you believe this?" She said to Him, "Yes, Lord, I believe that You are the Christ, the Son of God, who is to come into the world." (John 11.25-27)

Obviously, Jesus is not describing eternal biological life here. If so, Martha would still be with us--and nearing her 2000th birthday!

Rather, it seems that Jesus refers to two groups: The first group is composed of believers who would die before His "coming" (and the resurrection). Though they physically died, they would be raised and would "live" *spiritually.*

Secondly, since His Return and the Resurrection were to happen within that generation, Jesus comments on another group. The second group are those who would physically live past His "coming" (and the resurrection)--and, therefore, would "never die" *spiritually. They would not need resurrection!*

This is exactly what the apostle John promised Christians later on--those who lived within a very short time of Jesus' "coming":

> These things I have written to you who believe in the name of the Son of God, *that you may know that you have eternal life,* and that you may continue to believe in the name of the Son of God. (1 Jn. 5.13)

Notice, he said that they *"have eternal life"--present tense.* They were so close to the time of Jesus' "coming" that John describes them the way Jesus described the second group above--they would "never die".

This same teaching from Jesus is also found in another famous resurrection passage, John 5.24-30. Jesus, responding to some unbelieving Jews, said:

> "Most assuredly, I say to you, he who hears My word and believes in Him who sent Me *has everlasting life, and shall not come into judgment, but has passed from death into life.* Most assuredly, I say to you, the hour is coming, and now is, when *the dead will hear the voice of the Son of God; and those who hear will live.* For as the Father has life in Himself, so He has granted the Son to have life in Himself, and has given Him authority to execute judgment also, because He is the Son of Man. Do not marvel at this; for the hour is coming in *which all who are in the graves will hear His voice and come forth-those who have done good, to the resurrection of life, and those who have done evil, to the resurrection of condemnation.* I can of Myself do nothing. As I hear, I judge; and My judgment is righteous, because I do not seek My own will but the will of the Father who sent Me." (John 5.24-30)

First notice that Jesus alludes to Dan. 12.2 in verses 28-29, so we know that He refers to the same resurrection. Also, we see that these events were quite close: "the hour is coming, and now is."

Those who believed in Him would "not come into judgment," had "passed from death into life" and had "everlasting life." This is the second group of John 11--they would live past his Coming and would "never die."

The dead who would "hear the voice of the Son of God" would live--these are in the first group of John 11. Righteous Daniel would have been in this group.

But these are not the only dead to be raised and judged. Just as it was revealed to Daniel, some would experience the "resurrection of life"; others, the "resurrection of condemnation."

Paul's Resurrection Teaching

We have already noticed, in Paul's own words, that he taught the resurrection which was "written in the Law and in the Prophets" (Ac. 24.14), and which was the hope of Israel (Ac. 26.6). Thus, we will certainly expect Him to teach the same thing that Daniel (and Jesus) taught.

But first, a look at when Paul indicates it would take place. Paul, writing in the mid AD 50's, referring to the time of the resurrection said in 1 Cor. 15.51, *"We shall not all sleep"* (i.e. die, 1 Cor. 15.6). Thus, Paul places the time of the resurrection within the lifetime of some of his readers--certainly agreeing with the timeframe of Daniel and Jesus above.

Regarding the nature of the resurrection, Paul says it is *spiritual:*

> So also is the resurrection of the dead. The body is sown in corruption, it is raised in incorruption. It is sown in dishonor, it is raised in glory. It is sown in weakness, it is raised in power. It is sown a natural body, it is raised a *spiritual* body. There is a natural body, and there is a spiritual body. (1 Cor. 15.42-45)

So, Paul does, in fact, agree with Daniel and Jesus in his description of the *time* and *spiritual nature* of the resurrection.

Summary and Conclusion

We have learned that Jesus placed the time of His Coming and the Judgment within the lifetime of some of the apostles (Mt. 16.27-28). In Mt. 13.40, Jesus said that at His Coming, the Judgment (the harvest) would take place at the "end of *this* age"--which was the Mosaic Age (the only age in progress at that time).

When Jesus quoted Dan. 12.3 in Mt. 13.43, He linked the Resurrection to His Coming and the Judgment--because those described in that very verse were some who would be resurrected and judged.
We found that the end of the Mosaic Age was linked to the destruction of Jerusalem with its temple that symbolized the Old Covenant. (Mt. 24.1-3, 34; Dan. 9.26-27)

Thus, we concluded that the time of Jesus' Return, the Resurrection, and the Judgment was at the end of the Mosaic Age when Jerusalem was destroyed in AD 70.

Since this is true, we took a fresh look at the nature of these events in Scripture and realized that generally they were spiritual events described with figurative language.

Yet, we are sure that they took place because (1) we believe Jesus, and (2) we have a linked historical event--the destruction of Jerusalem and the temple--that verifies the occurrence of all of the unseen spiritual events at the "end of the age."

CHAPTER 3
Doctrinal Implications of Preterist Eschatology

Introduction

It is not enough to know *when* the Last Things were fulfilled; we also must understand *how* they were fulfilled and the *implications* of that fulfillment for us today. The "when" and "how" are continually being discussed in the pages of this and other preterist publications, but the doctrinal implications have not been sufficiently addressed. It is the purpose of this on-going series to focus on the doctrinal implications of the preterist view. In this introduction to the series, we will define some of the basic principles of preterist eschatology, suggest some possible implications and discuss ways to implement them. [6]

We realize a discussion of doctrinal issues can get complicated extremely fast, so we will attempt to provide explanations of any terms used that are not commonly understood. *Eschatology* comes from a Greek word which means "the last", so eschatology is the study of Last Things (i.e. events such as the return of Christ, the Resurrection, the Judgment, and our eternal destinies). The word *preterist* has general and specific meanings. The general definition refers to someone who believes most or all of Bible prophecy has been fulfilled sometime in the PAST, as opposed to a FUTURIST who affirms a yet future fulfillment of Bible prophecy. We use the term "preterist" in a more specific and limited sense, referring to those who believe all Bible prophecy was completely revealed and fulfilled about the time Jerusalem was destroyed in A.D. 70. Sometimes the preterist approach to Bible prophecy is labeled as "Realized Eschatology" (in the case of C. H. Dodd), "Fulfilled Eschatology" (by various preterist writers) or "Covenant Eschatology" (by Max King). Several among the Church of Christ group have also referred to the preterist view as "The A.D. 70 Theory."

---

[6] By Edward E. Stevens, http://www.preterist.org/articles/doctrinal_implications.asp, presented with permission. A few paragraphs have been left out to save space. It has no effect on the context of what Mr. Stevens has written. His email address is: preterist1@preterist.org

We plan to present only highlights and overviews in this series. Many books would not be enough to fully explain the Scheme of Redemption and its full implications. More details on each of the doctrinal implications are planned for forthcoming books.

Why Study Implications?

It is beneficial to re-examine our beliefs, even if we arrive at the same conclusions as before, because the exercise will help us better understand both *what* we believe and *why* we believe it. Far too many people barely know what they believe, much less why. Traditions should be re-studied by every generation, especially when deeper insights into the Scheme of Redemption are uncovered, *like what has happened now with spread of the preterist view.*

Is it consistent to want futurists to re-examine their eschatology, when we hesitate looking at how the preterist view might affect our other doctrines besides eschatology. Do we examine only those traditions we consider "non-essential" to fellowship? Or do we "examine everything" (1 Thess. 5:21) like the Bereans did (Acts 17:11), including our Sacred Cows?

Sometimes non-preterists perceive the implications more quickly and easily than preterists. Some, in fact, have already suggested that the preterist view affects much more than just our *timing* of the Last Things. For example, notice Almon Williams' comments at the 1986 Florida College Lectures ("A.D. 70: The End?" *The Doctrine of Last Things,* Melvin D. Curry, ed. 1986. p. 237):

The AD 70 view has been somewhat of an unstabilizing force in regard to what practices are to be continued after AD 70, for doubt has arisen in the minds of many regarding what firmly established pre-AD 70 practices were to continue to be practiced ... Some of the questioned practices have been the Lord's supper, elders, and even baptism. The problem is that a new point of emphasis is always unsettling at least for a time; in fact, one never knows how far others may apply his new issue, or how far, for that matter, he himself may finally be forced to go.

It is *unsettling* for some to hear it suggested that some of our cherished traditions may not be essential after 70 AD. But to others it is *liberating!* When evidence begins to surface that the preterist view affects other doctrines besides eschatology, we have an obligation to give it an objective look, even if it calls into question doctrines we consider essential.

Few could express the attitudes needed for such investigations any better than Max King did when he said to a group of preachers (April 22, 1971, quoted by Flavil Nichols in his lecture, "Max Kingism", *Premillennialism, True or False?* Wendell Winkler, ed. 1978. p. 98):

I'm just giving you my theory of it, my view on it. This is for you to think about; this is for you to study. I know it changes your views on a lot of things. It turns you around! It turned me upside down and every which way, even at night! (Laughter) You know, you get into something like this, and it bothers you! Really! But I've come to the conclusion that just simply because I'm a member of the Church of Christ has not guaranteed me that I possess and have all the truth. I've lost that concept, a long time ago. And I think this is one of our problems in the church: we fear (maybe) to look at a thing in a different view sometimes, lest it will show us that we have need of a change in a point of doctrine here or there along the way.

Indeed, the preterist view does "change our views on a lot of things". It has implications for many doctrines. Have we really gone so far in our study of the preterist view that we think we have seen all the implications, ramifications and logical extensions of it? Do we completely grasp the full impact of the preterist worldview upon all other Biblical doctrines besides eschatology (i.e. ecclesiology, soteriology, sacramentology, *et al)?* What if fulfilled eschatology does affect more than just our timing of the last things? Do the Reformation and Restoration movements stop with us? Are we really ready to lock out further study and crystallize into just another denomination? Or is there more yet to be explained? The search for an even better understanding needs to go on indefinitely. Further study should not be locked out, nor should the current state of understanding ever be made a test of fellowship. We need to find out how far these implications reach, and implement them into our lives and doctrinal systems. Not to do so is to blindly follow traditions which may or may not be Biblically correct.

Several of our readers have specifically asked us to deal with these doctrinal implications. Those who tend to have a strong, authoritarian institutional (church) framework may see this as an attack, while those outside the institutional (church) framework may believe we haven't gone far enough. We hope this series will provoke some fresh thinking and precipitate a better understanding of the Scriptures....

... What Do We Mean?

What exactly do we mean when we say we will be talking about the implications of the preterist view? Perhaps that is best answered by asking a few illustrative questions: Which of the teachings and examples found in the NT still apply to us after the consummation *of all things* about A.D. 70? If the *Preterist* view is correct, where does it leave us? What Biblical material is still applicable to us today? How does it affect the creeds, the organizational structure of the church, the sacraments, the continuation or cessation of charismatic gifts and a whole host of other doctrinal issues often taken completely for granted by *Futurists* (and some preterists as well)? What is the future of the world and the modern state of Israel? What rights, responsibilities and benefits do we have now since the Kingdom has arrived in its fullness? Is any part of the Mosaic Law still binding? Is it proper to bind upon believers today the things practiced in the period covered by the book of Acts (including the miraculous gifts)? Was there anything temporary and transitional about the church and its rituals that made them either get replaced by their spiritual counterparts, become no longer essential, or get done away with altogether about 70 AD? Do we already have the dominion that was promised? Is this dominion physically/materialistically-oriented, or spiritual in nature (a spiritual inheritance - the kingdom)? What role does hope play in the kingdom if prophecy has all been fulfilled? These are some of the implications we wish to address in this on-going series of articles.

Preterist Principles & Their Implications

We first list some basic Biblical principles (**boldfaced**) involved in preterist eschatology, and then suggest some possible implications. And we discuss how far these principles go, and how we implement them today. The implications will be more fully dealt with in the upcoming doctrinal series. Just because some implications and applications seem logically possible does not mean they are logically *necessary,* nor essential to put into practice. That is for you and I as individuals to discover for ourselves from our own study of God's Word. We simply suggest these ideas for your consideration.

1. The Kingdom Has Arrived. Daniel predicted the Kingdom would arrive in the days of the fourth beast (when the Hasmoneans and Romans controlled Judea). John and Jesus both said the Kingdom was "at hand" in their day. If the Kingdom is not here yet, then Daniel is a false prophet, along with John the Baptist and Jesus. After Pentecost the church did have a taste of those good things that were about to come, a pledge (earnest or down-payment) of the Kingdom blessings. But they did not inherit the fullness of the Kingdom until it was taken away from the apostate Jews about AD 70 and given to the true Israel composed of both the faithful Jewish remnant and the Gentiles (Rom. 2:28-29; 9:6; Gal. 3:7, 28-29; 6:16; Phil. 3:3). The fact that the Kingdom is here now speaks volumes against the bankrupt eschatology of the dispensational view with all their gaps, postponements, parentheses and failures of Christ to set up His "earthly" reign (a physical-literal paradise conjured up by the imagination of materialistic futurists). We are not just pessimistically occupying until it comes. It's here. We can live optimistically and victoriously in it right now and indefinitely into the future.

2. The Kingdom Is Spiritual. But how spiritual is it? How far do we go with this spiritual idea? Does this totally eliminate our involvement with physical things, or restrict us to just some physical things? Does it mean physical things have absolutely no meaning today, or a totally new spiritual meaning with no trace of the physical left behind? What did Jesus and Paul say the Kingdom really is? What is its nature? What is the kernel, the essence, the core, the real substance the Kingdom is made of? Obviously we still have physical bodies and live in a physical world, so the Kingdom must have some application to our physical life now IN the world (but not OF the world). Mk. 12:33, 34 Love for God and fellow man "is much more than all burnt offerings and sacrifices." This reveals much about the nature of the Kingdom.

3. The Kingdom must be entered and dwelt in through spiritual means. Can the Kingdom be entered by physical rituals, agreement to complex systems of man-made theology or only after the approval of powerful ecclesiastical institutions? It is obvious that it is entered spiritually. But is it only by spiritual means, or are there some physical rituals still mixed in? We will examine these questions in the upcoming article on "Sacramentology". A fleshly-oriented physical/literal interpretive method will miss the spiritual meaning of the kingdom. We need to change the way we approach the Bible. Our hermeneutical approach must be adjusted to the approach suggested by Paul in 1 Cor. 2:13-16 – the spiritual (not fleshly) approach to interpreting these things. The reason why most people miss the preterist view is because they are looking at things from a physical/literal "fleshly" point of view, rather than the spiritual perspective (see also 2 Cor. 4:18). This is the same mistake the Jews made when they crucified the Master. Paul frequently reminded the saints of his generation to set their minds on the heavenly things they already had a taste of and which were about to be (and now have been) fully consummated. If our focus is on the physical, fleshly things of the world, we have missed the Kingdom.

4. All things written about Christ in the OT have been fulfilled (Lk. 21:22) - As Jewish rabbis are prone to remind us, partial fulfillment just won't do. If Jesus didn't fulfill it all in His generation, then Jesus is not the Messiah. Not only does this mean the predictions about Christ have all come to pass, but it means that all the types that hinted of something fuller and better and more meaningful have blossomed as well. Roses in the bud may be beautiful to some, but they are nothing to compare with a rose in full bloom. The promise was a bud, and the fulfillment is like a rose in full bloom. Jesus came not to abolish the Law, but to *fulfill* (unveil its full meaning). The Law found its ultimate spiritual expression in Christ Jesus. And even though that old code of law is no longer binding in a national sense, its principles are still applicable to us.

5. Great Commission has been fulfilled (Matt. 28:18-20) - John the Baptist and Jesus were announcing the Good News about the soon arrival of the Kingdom. Jesus told them (Matt. 24:14) that this gospel would be *"preached in the whole world for a witness to all the nations"* before THE END (AD 70 destruction) came. And as far as we know all the apostles (except John) had died before the END of Judea and Jerusalem at A.D. 70. The good news about the near arrival of the Kingdom was fulfilled, just as Jesus predicted (Lk. 21:31). The kingdom has come. The gospel was spread to all the nations in that first generation, as Jesus had commanded. The terms of His great commission were fulfilled. So what are we preaching today? Are we still under obligation to announce the good news that the Kingdom is soon to arrive? No, we teach that the Kingdom is here now and lead others into it. Paul told Timothy (2 Tim. 2:2) to teach faithful men who would teach others (and so on). Faithful men will keep on teaching others, but not because we have been directly commissioned by Christ, but simply because we are being faithful to Christ in spreading the good news about the presence of our Redeemer and His victorious conquest over Satan, Sin and Death. A lot of sermon outlines about the Great Commission need to be adjusted in this regard.

6. All things have been made new (Rev. 21:5) - Does this just mean that *some* things were made *somewhat* new? Does this mean "new" in the sense of having never existed before, or does it mean that the "newness" that it once had has been restored (renewed, or made new again)? New in kind, or new in reference to time? Does Jesus' illustration of the new wine and old wineskins (Matt. 9:16, 17) have any application here? How much of the OT things were swept away to bring in the "new creation" of Christ (2 Cor. 5:17; Gal. 6:15). The question is, how do we tell what is old or transitional versus what is new and permanent? We will address these issues in several of the articles of the upcoming series.

7. The Scheme of Redemption Has Been Consummated. What does it mean when we say the scheme of redemption has been consummated? What did Adam and Eve lose? Was not the purpose of Christ to restore what was lost? Did He do it? Have we got that restored paradise, or are we still waiting for Him to redeem us from the curse? The Tree of Life (Rev. 2:7) has been restored. The serpent has been crushed (Rom. 16:20) and God's enemies defeated (1 Cor. 15:25; Lk. 19:27). The last enemy (death - 1 Cor. 15:26; Rev. 20:14) has been conquered. Final atonement for sin (Dan. 9:24) has been administered by the High Priest and He has returned out of the holiest place to announce that "salvation" has been consummated (Heb. 9:28). If we are living in the paradise of God again, does this mean that rituals, ceremonies, sacrifices (such as baptism, Lord's Supper, etc.), physical temples ("church" buildings), priesthood (clergy) and other such physical trappings are no longer "imposed" on us (see Heb. 9:10)? Adam and Eve didn't have those things in the Garden, nor did they need them until after the Fall and the Curse. Do we need those things now that the conditions of the Garden have been restored? But, do we go to the extreme of throwing them out with the proverbial "bath water", or could they still have some value if observed as teaching, confessional and tools of edification (even though no longer obligatory and binding)? See 2 Tim. 3:16-17.

8. Old Heavens and Earth Have Passed Away and the New Heavens and Earth Are Here (Matt. 5:17-20) – Jesus said, *"Do not think that I came to abolish the Law or the Prophets; I did not come to abolish, but to fulfill. For truly I say to you,* **until heaven and earth pass away, not the smallest letter or stroke shall pass away from the Law, until all is accomplished**. *Whoever then annuls one of the least of these commandments, and so teaches others, shall be called least in the kingdom of heaven; but whoever keeps and teaches them, he shall be called great in the kingdom of heaven. For I say to you, that unless your righteousness surpasses that of the scribes and Pharisees, you shall not enter the kingdom of heaven."* Have "heaven and earth" passed away? If not, are we still observing every jot and tittle of the Law? If the "heaven and earth" Jesus spoke of in this text still exists, then we are under obligation to both keep and teach it. But if the old heavens and earth have passed away, then the Law is no longer binding. The key word here is "binding" in distinction from "applicable." This does not mean the Law is no longer "applicable" or that it has nothing of value for kingdom dwellers today. The Law is still very useful, and we would do well to understand it as thoroughly as possible and APPLY its teachings to our life now in the Kingdom. But, the destruction of Jerusalem in AD 70 swept away the binding aspects of the old covenant (the old heavens and earth). A new heavens and earth (the kingdom) replaced those things (see Heb. 12:27,28). The priesthood, temple, sacrifices and law were changed into their spiritual counterparts (Heb. 7:12). We don't live under the Law now, because the better spiritual things of the new heavens and earth are here.

9. Time of Reformation Has Occurred (Heb. 9:10) - After talking about the temple, the priesthood, the sacrificial system, and the baptismal "washings" that were associated with the Law, the Hebrews writer says that all these things were "fleshly ordinances imposed until a time of reformation." Has that time of reformation occurred yet? It hadn't when the book of Hebrews was written, and that's one of the reasons why preterists say those "fleshly ordinances" were still "imposed" after Pentecost. Obviously they are no longer imposed on us today, so sometime between the writing of the book of Hebrews (about AD 60-65) and our day, the "time of reformation" must have occurred. What was this "time of reformation?" For those essential parts of the Law code to no longer be "imposed" would mean a radical change of some kind to the nation and governmental system that the Jews were familiar with. The most radical change in their whole national-religious history that would ever occur (according to Jesus in Mt. 24:21) was to be at the destruction of Jerusalem in AD 70. Is that the change the Hebrews writer had in mind? And what does that imply for all those fleshly ordinances (such as the baptismal "washings") that were "imposed" until that time of reformation? Are they still imposed? But, are they still "applicable" and useful as teaching and models of edification?

10. Christ Has Returned – He is here now to stay – He will never leave again. We will live in His presence forever. Jesus the High Priest has returned out of the Holy of Holies (heaven) to manifest the fact that Final Atonement has been made. How many times does Christ need to make atonement and come back out of heaven to proclaim it? The idea of multiple comings just doesn't fit the picture here (Hebrews 9). Now we have a better indwelling than what the transition period saints had. They had the miraculous indwelling and empowering of the Holy Spirit. We have Christ Himself dwelling with us and in us. And we no longer observe the Lord's supper as just a memorial of Him until He returns, but rather as a victory feast with Him at His table in His presence in His Kingdom now and forevermore. This certainly has implications for Pneumatology, Sacramentology and our worldview.

11. The "Perfect" Has Come (1 Cor. 13:10; Eph. 4:13) – We will not provide proof in this introductory article for our firm conviction that the miraculous gifts have passed away because we plan to do so in the article(s) dealing with Pneumatology. We simply assert that the "perfect" (or state of maturity and completeness) arrived by the time Jerusalem fell at AD 70, and so the miraculous gifts ceased at that time. This includes the gifts of leadership (cf. Eph. 4:11-13) as well as the gifts of prophecy, speaking in tongues and writing by inspiration. All inspired books were finished being written by that time. What are the implications of this cessation of miraculous gifts at AD 70? What does it mean when we say "the perfect has come"? What is included in the list of things that came to perfection or maturity or completion at AD 70? What if the leadership of the transition period church was miraculously endowed (cf. Eph. 4:7, 11)? And what if their authority as "overseers and shepherds" was based on this miraculous endowment (cf. Acts 20:28 "...the Holy Spirit has made you...")? If the miraculous gifts of leadership have ceased, how does this reflect on the supposed "authority" of church leaders today, especially if this "pattern" of leadership and organizational structure of the church was only temporary and merely designed to get them through the transition and tribulation period (AD 30-70) into the completely established state of maturity? Doesn't Eph. 4:11-13 teach that these gifts were for this purpose? And, doesn't this follow the same "pattern" in which other concerns were dealt with during that traumatic period; for instance the way Paul handled the issue of marriage and celibacy "in view of the present distress" (1 Cor. 7:26)? Jesus said that unless the tribulation of those days had been cut short no "flesh" (not even the "elect" remnant) would have been saved (Mt. 24:22). It was a very difficult time and required special gifts from the Holy Spirit (cf. Mt. 10:19, 20). So if the NT patterns of leadership and organizational structure of the church were temporary miraculously-given aids to get the church through that dangerous period of establishment, what does that imply for those who want to restore (and bind) those patterns of leadership today? How can it be valid to bind them today if the conditions that made them necessary during the transition period are not now here? And if the authority of that leadership was derived from the miraculous gifts which have ceased, how can leaders assume that kind of authority today? Wouldn't it be fair to say, at the very least, that those patterns of leadership and organizational structure are no longer binding upon us? This does not mean, however, that they are not applicable or useful or an edifying way to organize and expedite the work of teaching and caring for others. We are certainly free to do things that way. But the work of spreading the Kingdom does not depend on doing it that way today. If it did, the Kingdom could not spread in places like China where such leadership and organizational structure is illegal and impossible. Let's not bind where the Scriptures don't bind, nor loose where the Scriptures don't loose. Let's leave it in the area of expediency where the Scriptures do.

12. The Bridegroom has returned – The marriage has been consummated. What about those becoming Christians today, are they still being incorporated into the chaste bride who is yet to be married to Christ at His coming? If the bride has already married Christ, then who are we? Does this have any implications for the "church", the bride of Christ? Ecclesiology needs to take this concept into consideration.

13. The first covenant grew obsolete and disappeared (Heb. 8:13) – By the time Paul wrote his epistles, many of the OT things had already become obsolete and were no longer bound upon the brethren (see Rom. 14; Col. 2), and the rest were "ready to disappear" at 70 AD (Heb. 8:13). There are some very important spiritual principles for the Kingdom contained in Romans 14. Does it teach that we cannot bind holy days, dietary restrictions, rituals and other physical ordinances today? Each person has freedom to observe or not to observe those things. So then, observance becomes a matter of one's own expediency and edification. See Col. 2:16 also. It says not to let anyone act as our judge (either to force us to practice such things, or to forbid us from observing them). Is it possible that our requirements of observing the First Day of the week as a "Christian Sabbath", and the Lord's Supper, the tithe, and many other things like this are unnecessary? Re-read Rom. 14:5, 6 and think about the implications of those words for the church/kingdom today. Does he lay these things down as canon law, or leave them in the realm of expediency and edification (Rom. 14:17-19)?

14. The Mystery Is Finished (Rom. 16:25-26; 1 Cor. 2:6-8; Eph. 3:4-10; Rev. 10:7). One of the major stumbling-blocks of Christianity for the Jews has always been the notion that Gentiles could inherit God's kingdom blessings without becoming Jewish. Jesus alluded to the universal nature of the Kingdom numerous times in His parables and teachings. Apostle Paul especially brought this to sharp focus in the books of Romans and Ephesians where he plainly stated that the universal aspect of the Kingdom (both Jew and Gentile) was then being revealed and established. It is something which we take for granted today, but which in Bible times was not clearly understood almost until the End. The Kingdom is composed of both Jew and Gentile today, and access to the Kingdom is no longer restricted by racial or nationalistic barriers. So, obviously the mystery which Paul referred to has been consummated. We are all (both Jew and Gentile) one in Christ. Teaching that the mystery (i.e. Rev. 10:7) is still yet to be consummated (as dispensationalists do) undermines the integrity of both Christ and Scripture. God saved both Jews and Gentiles and restored His fellowship with all mankind through Christ. This was not easy for the Jews to accept, but this was the mystery that was planned before the ages, revealed throughout their redemptive history and consummated in Christ. Since it has been consummated, we know the rest of the Last Things have occurred as well, because they were all intimately connected with the administration of the mystery which would see "the summing up of all things" (Eph. 1:10). So if the mystery has been totally revealed and consummated in Christ, how can we give ear to the Zionist contention that their racial and national identity must be preserved and perpetuated in order to fulfill Bible prophecy?

15. Death and Hades have been thrown into the Lake of Fire (Rev. 20:13-14). Christ is victorious. His plan to redeem man from sin and death has triumphed. Satan and his sons (Mt. 12:34; John 8:44) made one last attempt to wipe out God's people in the persecution throughout the period of the book of Acts, but they were no match for the sinless sacrifice of the God-man Jesus. Death (the last enemy) has been conquered through the spiritual and eternal life that we now have in Christ. The gates of Hades did not prevail. The old waiting place where the dead awaited the final drama of the scheme of redemption has been emptied of its contents and done away with forever. Now when we die physically we continue living spiritually in the presence of God (except without our physical bodies). We do not have to go to some waiting place, be resurrected, reunited with our physical bodies, judged and then changed back into some non-material state in which to spend eternity. When we became Christians we passed out of judgment and death into eternal spiritual life.

16. All things have been "restored" (Acts 3:21) - What did Peter have in mind when he mentioned this "restoration of all things" (Acts 3:21) in connection with the return of Christ (Acts 3:20)? It is also referred to in this context as "times of refreshing" (3:19) and being "blessed" with the Abrahamic blessings (3:25, 26). Peter also stated to those Jews that they must "repent" (3:19) and "give heed to everything" Jesus had taught (3:22). Those who did not heed Christ would be "utterly destroyed" (3:23). It recalls the "blessing and cursing" covenant language of OT passages like Lev. 26 and Deut. 28. And one other note: Peter wasn't talking about some far away time for all of these events to happen, since he says these events, spoken of by all the prophets, referred to "these days" in which Peter lived (3:24). So, what has been restored? The blessings that God promised Abraham would come upon all the families of the earth. Was this to be a restoration of Mideast property and national government system? According to Apostle Paul (Rom. 9:6-8; Gal. 3:7-14; 3:29; 4:5-7) they were heirs of "every spiritual blessing in the heavenly places in Christ" (Eph. 1:3-14) and were to inherit throughout the "ages to come" all the "surpassing riches of His grace" (Eph. 2:7). These were the blessings of Abraham, the "better country" (Heb. 11:16), the "heavenly Jerusalem" (Heb. 12:22) and the "kingdom which cannot be shaken" (Heb. 12:28), where "the water of life" and "the tree of life" are freely available (Rev. 22:1, 2). That unshakable kingdom and heavenly city is ours today. Paradise has been restored. We have all the spiritual blessings that were promised to Adam and Eve, Noah, Abraham, David and all the other patriarchs (Heb. 11-13). So why do so many Christians just continue to pessimistically eke out an existence thinking the "better things" will only be theirs after they die? We've got them in our possession now while in our physical bodies as well as after we die physically and continue on in His presence in the heavenly kingdom. This principle has heavy implications for an optimistic worldview that is right for the Christian both in his relationship with the world and with his fellow Christian. And, it is the right view for the information age and the global village now and into the future.

17. Armageddon is past. The Anti-Christ has already come and gone. The Tribulation is over. The Rapture has occurred. All of the final events of the Last Days have been fulfilled. The Last of the Last Days (the end) of the Dominion of Sin and Death (the Domain of Satan and his sons, Mt. 12:34; John 8:44) has already come and gone. So what is left in our future? Are there any pessimistic events to dread, which Jesus hasn't given us victory over. Preterists are the only ones who can have a consistently optimistic worldview both now and for the indefinitely long future ahead.

Conclusion

As we have seen, the possible implications of the preterist approach touch some very important doctrinal areas. Since we have only just begun to explore the implications, it is impossible to say how many doctrines are either directly or indirectly affected by the preterist view. But, what we have seen so far suggests that it has implications for every important area of theological study, and for every segment of "Christendom" including the Catholic, Orthodox, Protestant, Reformed, Restoration, Reconstruction, Charismatic and Messianic Hebrew Christian movements, as well as the cults and fringe groups who still traffic in Sabbath observance, festivals, and other physically-oriented rituals, ceremonies and traditions. We are not attacking any particular denomination or movement, but simply encouraging all of us to take a second look at our traditional doctrinal positions in light of the preterist view.

How far do these implications go? It depends on how far it is *necessary* to take them, and how far we are *willing* to take them, in order to apply them to the culture we are a part of. Cultural factors quite often determine how expedient the spread of the Kingdom will be. The Scriptures are more flexible than most Christians realize (because of these cultural differences). They have been taken to some radically different extremes. That does not become a serious problem unless the extreme position becomes exclusive toward all other views. It is this exclusivism, not the extremism, that is the real threat to Christian unity and the spread of the Kingdom. There is room in the Kingdom for a lot of cultural diversity and freedom of opinion...

... Please give us your feedback. What implications of the preterist view do you see? Write to the attention of: *The Editor, International Preterist Association, 122 Seaward Ave., Bradford, PA 16701.*

CHAPTER 4
Matthew 24 Explained[7]

The importance of this passage to the *millennia and the Preterist* is indicated by his frequent reference to it, especially to the "signs of the times." While it is obviously a difficult passage, two or three verses are keys to a correct understanding of the chapter. This emphasizes the importance of studying any passage in the light of its context.

Most Preterist that I have studied develop their theology by combining Matthew 24 and 25 into one thought process. Which is the case with Mr. Petty's previous essay. Therein lies much of their misunderstanding of Holy Writ. *[This paragraph added by Morris Bowers]*

The Chapter Provides a Key to the Time of Its Fulfillment

The key to understanding the chapter and making a proper application of the "signs of the times" is found in verses 34-36.

A. "This generation shall not pass away, till all these things are accomplished" (verse 34). This verse serves to divide the chapter into two main divisions:

   1. Concerning the destruction of Jerusalem (Matt. 24:1-35).
   2. Concerning the end of the world (Matt. 24:36-51).

B. The expression "this generation" refers to the generation that was living at the time Jesus spoke.

   1. Consider how the word" generation" is used in other passages in the book of Matthew: (cf. Matt. 11:16; 12:38-45; 16:4; 23:36).
   2. The Jehovah's Witnesses want to make it a generation that began in 1914. "This generation" indicates a generation that was contemporary with Jesus.

---

[7] James E. Cooper, The Kingdom of God vs. Millennialism, October 2001, Cooper Publications

C. In the statement, "Heaven and earth shall pass away, but My words will by no means pass away" (verse 35), Jesus assured the disciples of the certainty of His prophecies. What He said would happen!

D. Verse 36 indicates a different time than that referred to in verses 1-35. "But of that day and hour no one knows, no, not even the angels of heaven, but My Father only.

▶ The expression "that day and hour" is used elsewhere in the New Testament in reference to the time of Christ's Second Coming and final judgment of all men (cf. Matt. 7:22; 11:22; Jno. 5:28-29; 1 Thess. 5:2; 2 Thess. 1:10; 2 Tim. 1:12, 18; 4:8).

▶ Please notice that it is day [singular], in contrast to days [plural] as used in the first thirty-five verses of the chapter.

▶ The following chart will demonstrate the contrast that the Lord is making between the destruction of Jerusalem (24:1-35) and His Second Coming (24:36-51).

DESTRUCTION OF JERUSALEM	CHRIST'S SECOND COMING
Section (1) Matt. 24:1- 35	Section (2) Matt. 24: 36-51
1- Definite Signs to Precede	1- Indefinite—"Know Not"
2- Time Unusual; Wars & Pestilence	2- Normal—Marrying, Famines, Working
3- Fig Tree—Gives Warning	3- Thief—Gives no Warning
4- No Delay	4- Delay—Evil Servant, Virgins, Talents (25: 1-30)
5- Local Judgment, Jerusalem, Judea	5- Universal Judgment, All Nations & People
6- Judgment on Earth	6- Judgment in Heaven

Jesus Is Answering Questions of the Disciples.

The question of the disciples was in response to His prediction that the Temple would be destroyed: "Not one stone shall be left here upon another, that shall not be thrown down" (Matt. 24:2).

1. The disciples ask: "When will these things be? And what will be sign of Your coming, and of the end of the world?" (Matt. 24:3).

2. An examination of the parallel passages reveals that the disciples wanted to know two things (cf. Mark 13:4; Luke 21:7).

a. "Tell us, when will these things be?"

b. "And what sign will there be when these things are about to take place?" (Luke 21:7)... "the sign when all these things will be fulfilled" (Mark 13:4).

3. It seems quite apparent that in the minds of the disciples the destruction of the temple would be the end of the world; i.e., the end of all things. They could not envision one without the other.

Whatever confusion there may have been in their minds, Jesus divides the answer into two parts:

1. He speaks of the destruction of the city and the Temple, the signs, *by which it could be foreseen,* and showing it would occur before that generation passed away (Matt. 24:3-35).

2. He then spoke of His Second Coming, the end of the present dispensation, explaining that there is no sign, and only the Father knows when this would take place (Matt. 24:36-51).

The Signs of the Impending Destruction of Jerusalem.

A. False Teachers (vs. 5). Various Jewish insurrection leaders attempted to bolster their claims by pretending to be the Christ. Josephus, the Jewish historian of the first century, verifies that there were many who made such a claim near the time of Jerusalem's fall in AD 70. Simon the sorcerer (Acts 8) made such pretensions prior to his conversion.

B. Wars and Rumors of Wars (vs. 6). Revolts broke out in every part of the Roman Empire among smaller nations prior to AD 70. Moreover, there were wars among the Jews themselves, agitated by zealots, and these intensified as the siege of Jerusalem began (cf. Josephus).

C. Famine and Pestilence (vs. 7). Acts 11:28 refers to one extensive famine which occurred in the days of Claudius Caesar. Another famine affecting Jerusalem occurred about 15 years later (cf. Josephus).

D. Earthquakes (vs. 8). Great earthquakes occurred during the reign of Nero (AD 54-68). Many places experienced, or were destroyed by, earthquakes: Crete, Miletus, Chios, Samos, Laodicea, Hierapolis, Smyrna, Colosse, Campania, Rome and Judea.

E. Persecution of the Church (vs. 9-13). Began with the stoning of Stephen (Acts 7). The church in Jerusalem was scattered (Acts 8). James was killed and Peter was imprisoned by Herod (Acts 12); Paul was arrested and shamefully treated (Acts 16 and 20-28). Many were offended, false teachers arose, and the love of many did wax cold (vs. 10-12). Some, like Phygellus and Hermogenes, turned away from the truth (2 Tim. 1:15). Demas forsook Paul, "having loved this present world" (2 Tim. 4:10). There are many references in the Epistles to false teachers, exhortations to faithfulness, and rebukes for the lack of faithfulness during this period.

   1. "But he that shall endure unto the end, the same shall be saved" (vs. 14).

   2. This was not a reference to final salvation, but to the deliverance of the faithful from the destruction which was to come when Jerusalem fell. By their careful watching for these signs, they were to know when to flee.

F. Gospel to All the World (vs. 14). The literal fulfillment of such is declared in Rom. 10:15-18 and Col. 1:23. These books were written before the destruction of Jerusalem [Romans, AD 56; Colossians, AD 61].

   1. Note: "and then the end will come," refers to the end of Jerusalem and its Temple, not to the end of the world.

2. Whenever a person projects the fulfillment of these signs to a time yet future, he completely ignores the Lord's statement that these things would happen before the passing of that generation.

Signs to Indicate the Fall of Jerusalem was Near.

When the disciples observed these signs, they were to know that the time of the destruction of the city was upon them and they should flee to the mountains for safety.

A. Abomination of Desolation (vs. 15). This refers to the raising of the Roman standards and idolatrous symbols in the holy place of the temple "where they ought not to be" (cf. Luke 21:20-21).

B. Disciples Flee (vs. 16-20). When the Roman troops began to surround the city, the disciples were to take that as a sign to flee to the mountains. If on the housetop when they saw the advancing troops, they were not to stop to gather any possessions out of the house (vs. 17). Those in the fields were not to return to their houses for their property (vs. 18). The reason for such haste was that life was more valuable than property. Such a time would work a hardship on mothers with nursing children (vs. 19). If it came in the winter, there was risk of exposure; if it came on a Sabbath Day, the gates of the city would be closed (vs. 20).

1. What sense does this paragraph make if interpreted to refer to the Second Coming of Christ?

2. What difference would it make if He came in the winter or on a Sabbath Day?

3. What good would it do for men to flee into the mountains?

C. Great Tribulation (vs. 21). "This is a strong statement to attach to the destruction of an earthly city. Yet, no one could read the historical accounts of this overthrow in Josephus without realizing how this applied to that destruction. The siege of the city, cutting off food supplies, and the hope of any outside help reaching them, led to starvation and every kind of disease which accompanies such a time. It is reported that people actually ate their own children. Jews murdered their fellow sufferers in order to plunder their houses in search of food. Then, when the Romans did come in, they slaughtered Jews in droves in the streets so that blood ran as a mighty current through the streets. Josephus reports that over a million and a quarter Jews were slain. Even allowing for his tendency to exaggerate, there must have been a terrible slaughter. It was more terrible by virtue of the fact that it was a divine judgment upon a people who had rejected their only hope of salvation." (Connie W. Adams, *Premillennialism,* page 13).

D. Days Shortened (vs. 22). Mercifully, the siege was short, and at one point was suspended to be finally executed under Titus, the Roman general.

E. Pseudo-signs (vs. 23-26). The Jews expected the Christ to appear and rescue them; excitement and rumors ran rampant among them.

F. The Eagles and the Carcass (vs. 27-28). The Son of Man was coming in judgment by means of the Roman armies. The Romans were the "eagles" [vultures] and Jerusalem was the "carcass." Thus, the destruction of the city of Jerusalem is pictured as the devouring of a carcass by hungry vultures. No wonder the Lord wept as He saw the coming destruction. These verses describe the swiftness of the occurrences connected with the siege of Jerusalem.

The Immediate Consequences of the Siege of Jerusalem.

A. There are some who apply the first part of the chapter to the destruction of Jerusalem, but make these verses apply to the Second Coming of Christ. This interpretation ignores two facts:

1. Verse 34 embraces this paragraph (vs. 29-33) as much as the rest of the chapter down to this point. Whatever was meant in these verses, that generation would not pass until it was fulfilled.

2. Verse 29 says **"immediately after the tribulation of these days."** Events happening many hundreds of years later would not be immediately after those days.

B. *Signs in the Heavens* (vs. 29). This is figurative language, and was used several times in the Old Testament to depict the downfall of nations, powers and dignitaries (cf. Isaiah 13:10; Ezekiel 32:7-8; Jeremiah 15: 7). If the fall of Babylon could be described by such language, surely the downfall of Jerusalem could be predicted with such. The light of Judaism was going out. Her sun would set, never to rise again. Her reflected honor in her dignitaries would shine no more.

C. *The Coming of the Son of Man* (vs. 30). Christ came in power in the transpiring of the events surrounding the destruction of Jerusalem-the events being a testimony that in spite of Jewish efforts to destroy Him, He was in heaven on the throne (cf. Matt. 26:64).

D. *Send forth Angels* (vs. 31). "Angels" here refers to "messengers" (cf. Matt. 11:10), and the reference is to the spread of the gospel to the four corners of the earth [universally] following the fall of Jerusalem. With the hindrance of Judaism removed, a great advance in the progress of the gospel was made throughout the world.

E. *Parable of the Fig Tree* (vs. 32-33). Just as they could know summer was nigh when the branches of the fig tree put forth leaves, even so they could know the fall of Jerusalem was near when they saw the predicted signs.

No "Sign" to Announce the End of the World.

A. Circumstances approaching the end of the world will be like those approaching the flood in the time of Noah (vs. 37-39).

1. By the preaching of Noah mankind had been warned about the coming destruction, but they paid no heed (cf. 2 Peter 2:5).

2. They continued with "life as usual," eating, drinking, marrying, giving in marriage-ordinary pursuits of life.

3. Those who believed the Word of God made preparations; and those who scoffed at it made no preparations (cf. 2 Peter 3:5-7).

B. The situation in Noah's day illustrates what will take place when the Lord comes again (vs. 40-42).

    1. "One is taken and the other is left." This refers to their salvation.

    2. Just as in the days of Noah many people will be caught unprepared at the end of the world and the day of judgment.

    3. Even the closest of human relationships will be severed at 'His coming.

C. Constant watchfulness is required if we are to be ready when the Lord Comes again (vs. 42-44).

    1. We do not know at what hour the Lord comes (vs. 41).

    2. If we knew when it would be, we would be prepared for Him like we would be prepared for a thief if we knew when he was coming.

D. Several illustrations are then given by Jesus to illustrate the principle of preparedness (Matt. 24:45 thru Chapter 25.

    1. The "signs of the times" were fulfilled in the destruction of Jerusalem in AD 70.

    2. There will be no "signs" leading up to the Second Coming of Christ. We must maintain a constant state of preparedness.

    3. Don't allow yourself to think that you have "time enough yet."

Realized Eschatology

Matthew 24	Luke 21:5-33
When Shall These Things Be?	**What Shall Be The Sign of Thy Coming?**
False Teachers, v5 (Acts 5:36-37)	No sign given; only Father knows
Wars, v6 (Josephus)	No man or angel knows, vs.36
Famines, Earthquakes, v7 (Acts 11:28-30)	n/a
Kill you, v9 (Peter, Paul, James, Acts 12:1ff)	**As days of Noah, Vs38-42**
Many Offended, v20	Every-day affairs, v3
Persecutions, v11	Illustration, vs. 40-42
Gospel Preached, v14, (Col 1:23)	
End Coming: Destruction of Jerusalem	**Three-Fold Warning, vs. 43-44**
Abomination of Desolation, v15 (Lk.21:20)(A Roman Symbol)	Be Ye Ready—Make Preparation
Disciples to Flee, vs 16-20, (Lk. 21:20-24)	As you Think Not—A Surprise
Great Tribulation, vs 20-28 (Fall of Jerusalem)	Son of Man is Coming—Certainty
After Tribulation, vs. 29-30 (Darkness of Jewish Nation)	A- A Promise, Acts 1:11 B- As Thief in Night, 2 Peter 3:10
Coming of the Son of Man, v30 (Not the Second Coming)	C- End of World, 2 Peter 3:10 D- Resurrection of All The Dead., (John 5:28-29; 11:24; "Last Day"
Angels Gather the Elect, v31 (Messengers—Gospel Spreads)	E- Judgment, John 12:48; "Last Day" Matt.25:31-46 F- Kingdom Delivered to God, (1 Cor. 15:24-25)
GENERATION NOT PASS TILL ALL THESE THINGS BE FULFILLED! Vs.33-34	**NO PROOF THAT CHRIST WILL SET FOOT ON EARTH AGAIN!**
VERSE 34 SETTLES "THE SIGNS"	**VERSE 36 SETTLES "THE COMING"**

The "Key" that Unlocks Chapter 24[8]

Occasionally, in a context characterized by some difficulty, there will be a "key" passage that unlocks the meaning of the material (cf. 1 Corinthians 7:26). Such is the case with reference to Matthew 24. The significant verse is thirty-four, wherein the Lord states:

> Verily I say unto you, this generation shall not pass away, till all these things be accomplished (ASV).

Before giving consideration to some of the details of this verse, let us make a general observation. When there are several passages that deal with a topic, some of which are clearer than others, or some of which are framed in language more literal than others, the less-ambiguous, or more literal, are to be employed as the guiding force in the interpretation. This is fundamental exegetical procedure.

Now here is the point: Matthew 24:34 is a **clear, literal statement** from the Lord relative to the events previously discussed. This text, therefore, **must** be a prevailing guideline in the interpretation of this inspired narrative.

Crucial to understanding this verse, and the context overall, is the term "generation." The Lord clearly indicated that "this" generation, i.e., **his** generation, would not "pass away," until the events depicted in verses 4-33 were "accomplished," i.e., fulfilled.

It has been common for dispensationalists to identify "generation" (Greek *genea*) with the Jewish race, hence to contend that "the family of Israel" will be preserved until all "these things" are fulfilled (Scofield, 1945, 1034). Since the Jewish people are still extant, this concept allows dispensationalists to stretch the circumstances of Matthew 24 all the way to the present time. This view of the passage is seriously flawed.

While millennialists argue that *genea* means "race" in rare instances,

---

[8] Wayne Jackson, www.christiancourier.com/articles/19-a-study-of-matthew-24

some of them acknowledge that this is not the "more common and usual meaning of the word" (Archer 1982, 339). Certainly there is no indication that *genea* is ever employed in the sense of "race" in the Gospel of Matthew – perhaps in the entire New Testament.

Genea is found forty-three times in the New Testament. In seventeen of these cases, the expression is "this generation." In Matthew's record, for example, "this generation" is found in 11:16; 12:41,42,45; 23:36, and 24:34. A careful consideration of these passages provides a clear sense of the significance of the expression.

For instance, Jesus, surveying the Jewish wickedness of his day, warned of an impending punishment. He said:

> "All these things [the consequences of the Jews' rebellion] shall come upon **this generation**" (Matthew 23:36; emp. added).

Why is it millennialists contend that "this generation" in 23:36 is the generation devastated by the Romans in A.D. 70, but allege that "this generation" in 24:34 refers to a far-away "future day" (Barbieri, 1983, 75,78)?

Arndt and Gingrich suggest that *genea* denotes "basically, the sum total of those born at the same time, expanded to include all those living at a given time generation, contemporaries" (1967, 153).

McClintock and Strong state that the phrase "this generation" in Matthew 24:34 denotes "the generation of persons then living contemporary with Christ" (1969, 776).

Herodotus, the Greek historian, said that "three generations" fill up a "century" (*The Histories* II.142). To him, a "generation" was a period of some thirty-three years.

It should be obvious that the events of Matthew 24:4-34 have to do with the generation that was contemporary with the Lord. The Christians could look for certain tell-tale indicators, detailed by the Savior, and "know" that the Lord's judgment upon Jerusalem was near (v. 33).

But of "that [the] day" of the Son's final coming, "knoweth no one" except the Father (v. 36). There is thus a **clear contrast** between Christ's temporal activity, chronicled prior to verse thirty-four, and that of the Lord's judgment at the end of time.

Jerusalem's Destruction

As Jesus left the environs of the sacred area, his disciples directed attention to the temple. The Lord declared that this edifice would be "thrown down" so that not one stone would be left upon another (24:2). There is no doubt but that Jesus was uttering an oracle concerning the destruction of the city by the Romans (cf. Matthew 22:7; Luke 21:20).

Later, on the Mount of Olives, the disciples asked: "When shall these things [the demolition of the temple] be?" They also wanted to know what would be the "sign" of his "coming, and of the end of the world" (24:3).

R.C. Foster has well observed:

> Much of the confusion in interpreting the predictions of Jesus recorded in Matthew 24 and the parallel passages arises from the failure to see that the disciples asked and Jesus answered two questions: one, concerning the fall of Jerusalem; the other, concerning His second coming (1971, 1187).

The disciples likely assumed that the destruction of the temple, and the end of the world, would occur at the same time. The Master sought to correct that impression, first, by discussing the Roman invasion (vv. 4-34), and then by commenting regarding his final coming to render universal judgment (vv. 35-51).

Jesus gave a series of clues which could be used by first-century saints to determine when Judaism's fall would occur. A brief survey of these is as follows (see vv. 5-14):

1. False "messiahs" would arise.

2. There would be numerous military encounters.

3. Famines and earthquakes would occur.

4. Disciples would be persecuted.

5. Some would "stumble," i.e., depart from the faith.

6. False prophets would be prevalent.

7. Decreasing spirituality on the part of some saints would be evident.

8. Those who endured would be delivered.

9. The gospel would be published far and wide during these four decades.

As unlikely as some of these prophetic declarations may seem to the skeptic, each of them was fulfilled by the time Jerusalem fell in A.D. 70. A more thorough discussion of these matters may be found in J. Marcellus Kik's volume, *Matthew 24*.

Continuing, Christ declared that the impending invasion had been foretold in the book of Daniel (chapter fifteen). The Savior thus urged the disciples to be ready to flee the city, praying that God would providentially accommodate their departure (Matthew 24:16-19).

He described the intensity of the Roman assault and promised that God would intervene for "the elect's" sake (vv. 21-22). The disciples were not to be swayed by false claims that Jesus had personally arrived, because, when that event actually occurred, it would be globally evident (vv. 23-27).

The Jewish nation was described as a rotting carcass where birds of prey would gather (v. 28). The fall of the Hebrew system is set forth in the sort of apocalyptic nomenclature that is characteristic of Old Testament literature, e.g., when the prophets pictorially portray the overthrow of Jehovah's enemies (cf. Isaiah 13:10-11; 34:2ff; Ezekiel 32:7-8).

All of this would be a "sign" of the fact that "the Son of man in heaven" was orchestrating these events (vv. 29-30). It is important to observe that the Lord would be accomplishing "these things" **from heaven**, not from some position upon the earth. The result of Judaism's demise would be a great gospel harvest, reminiscent of the Jubilee celebration of Old Testament fame (v. 31; cf. Luke 4:17-21).

Finally, just as the ancient citizen of Palestine could determine the coming of summer by the budding of the fig tree, even so, by reflecting upon the signals given by Christ, the disciples would be able to discern the approach of the promised calamity (vv. 32-33).

The "Signs" of Matthew Twenty-four

Our major thrust now will be to argue the case that the "signs" of Matthew 24:4ff **do not** find their fulfillment in the final return of Christ.

First, whereas dispensationalists argue for a 20th century fulfillment of these signs, accompanied by a nuclear holocaust (Lindsey 1970, 135-57), contextual indicators clearly reflect the fact that Jesus had reference to an **ancient and local situation**. Consider the following factors.

1. The impending destruction would involve the Jewish temple – "the holy place" (24:15), and the city of Jerusalem (Luke 21:20)—not New York, Paris, etc., as alleged by Lindsey and others. The temple has lain in ruins for more than nineteen centuries, and there is no evidence that it will ever be rebuilt.

2. The Jerusalem disciples were warned to flee unto the mountains (v. 16)—hardly efficacious advice if a nuclear attack were envisioned. However, the early Christians understood this admonition, and fled to Pella, beyond the Jordan, when the Romans advanced toward the city (*Eusebius History* III.5).

3. Christ warned: "Let him that is on the housetop not go down to take out the things that are in his house" (v. 17).

Again, such instruction hardly would be appropriate under the conditions of a nuclear assault. "On the house top" is the last place one would want to be! But the admonition made perfect sense in view of the fact that the houses of old Jerusalem were flat-roofed and situated close to one another. Accordingly, Christians might proceed, by way of "the road of roofs," to the edge of the city, thus escaping the invading soldiers (Edersheim 1957, 93).

4. Jesus urged: "Pray ye that your flight be not in the winter" nor "on a sabbath" (v. 20). This anticipates primitive conditions when winter travel could be rigorous; moreover, the gates of Jerusalem would be closed on the Sabbath (Nehemiah 13:19), which would make escape more difficult.

Second, though the destruction of Jerusalem was seen as a sort of "coming" of Christ (cf. Matthew 10:23; 24:30,33; Luke 21:27), i.e., in **judgment** upon the Hebrew nation—such was emphatically distinguished from the event known as the "second" coming (cf. Hebrews 9:28). The Lord cautioned that if any false teacher should attempt to proclaim his visible coming in connection with Jerusalem's fall, the bogus prophet was to be ignored, because the second coming would be apparent **universally** (vv. 23-27), whereas the destruction of Jerusalem was but a **local event**. Jerusalem's fall would only reflect a sign of Christ's providential coming in destructive judgment upon the holy city (vv. 29-31), not the Savior's visible, final coming. More on this momentarily.

Third, it is very significant that the Lord, in connection with his discussion of the destruction of Jerusalem, introduced the remarkable prophecy that had been given five centuries earlier to the prophet Daniel. Jesus said:

> When therefore ye see the abomination of desolation, which was spoken of through Daniel the prophet, standing in the holy place (let him that readeth understand), then let them that are in Judea flee (24:15,16).

The dispensational theory argues that the "abomination of desolation" is, from our vantage point, yet in the future. Supposedly, the prophetic focus is upon "the Antichrist," alleged to be "a world dictator" who will "make the temple abominable" in the so-called "Tribulation" period just prior to the Lord's second coming (Barbieri 1983, 77). The problem with this view is this: Daniel connects the appearance of the "abomination that makes desolate" with the **first** coming of Christ, not the Lord's **second** coming (9:24-27)!

The Prophecy of Daniel's Seventy Weeks

Let us, in this connection, briefly examine this fascinating prophecy. There is a three-fold thrust to the narrative.

First, it foretells the "Anointed" One's advent, and what would be accomplished thereby. The Messiah would: finish transgression, bring an end to sins, make reconciliation for iniquity, usher in everlasting righteousness, seal up vision and prophecy, be anointed as the most holy one, make firm a new covenant, and terminate sacrifices.

These things are associated with Christ's redemptive work at Calvary—not his second coming. To suggest that Daniel's prophecy contains a "long parenthesis," the "church age" (between the sixty-ninth and seventieth weeks), which was wholly unknown to the Old Testament prophets, is without any rational basis.

Second, the prophecy sets forth a chronological time-frame in which the messianic events would take place. From the time of Judah's commission to leave Babylonian captivity (in 457 B.C.), some 486-1/2 years (set forth in three increments—with "days" signifying "years") would pass, thus terminating in the very year of Jesus' death.

Finally, the terrible price for the Jews' rejection of Jesus is graphically portrayed.

> As a result or consequence of the death of the Messiah one making desolate (i.e. the Roman prince Titus) appears "upon the wing of abominations" (i.e. the pinnacle of the temple). By this language the complete destruction of the temple is signified (Young, 679).

It is not without significance that the Jews themselves recognized that the destruction of Jerusalem in A.D. 70 was the fulfillment of Daniel's prophecy. Josephus, the Jewish historian, stated that "Daniel also wrote concerning the Roman government, and that our country should be made desolate by them" (*Antiquities of the Jews* 10.11.7). This view of "Daniel's seventy weeks," commonly called the "traditional" view, "has been held with slight variation by most Biblical scholars until recent years" (Scott 1975, 364).

Jesus' Discussion of His Second Coming

Beginning in verse thirty-five, the Lord turns his attention to the final day of history, the day of his ultimate "coming." Heaven and earth will pass away, but the Savior's words will remain inviolate.

Jesus shows that there had been a broad range of indicators—"all these things"—which, when observed, would allow the Christians to escape the horrible Roman invasion (v. 33). Nevertheless, at the time of the second coming, no such signs would be provided; rather, the end of the world will occur in a dramatically unannounced fashion. Let us study some of the Lord's arguments.

The Savior affirmed:

> But of that day and hour knoweth no one, not even the angels of heaven, neither the Son, but the Father only (v. 36).

First, observe the use of "but," an adversative particle, which stresses a contrast between the previous material and that which follows. Professor Kik comments that this verse "gives immediate evidence of a change in subject matter" (1984, 101). In verses four through thirty-four the Lord had spoke of the "days" (plural) of tribulation associated with Jerusalem's peril (vv. 19, 22, 29), but now it is "the day" (singular)—an expression commonly used of the final day of history (cf. 1 Corinthians 3:13; 1 Thessalonians 5:4; 2 Timothy 1:12).

Second, observe that even Jesus himself did not know when "the day" of his coming (cf. v. 36) would be. Yet, he had given signs whereby others might "know" (v. 33) that he was providentially "nigh" in the destruction of Jerusalem. Obviously the two events were not the same.

Is it not rather ironical that Christ, who gave these "signs," did not know (while on earth) when his return would take place, but modern dispensationalists can read Matthew 24 and virtually pinpoint the time of the second coming! In 1992 Harold Camping, a syndicated television preacher, wrote:

> The results of this study indicate that the month of September of the year 1994 is to be the time for the end of history (1992, 531).

Third, Christ cited an historical example which demonstrated that those of the pre-flood world were unaware of their impending doom "until the flood came, and took them all away." The point being, "so shall be the coming of the Son of man" (v. 39). There will be no specific, chronological warning!

Fourth, Jesus appealed to certain cultural circumstances to depict the sudden, unanticipated nature of his return. Two men would be working in the field; one would be taken, the other left (v. 40). Two women will be grinding at the mill; one is taken, one is left (v. 41). Then, in a parallel reference, two men are in bed; one is taken, the other is left" (Luke 17:34).

One scholar has observed that these references contemplate different times of the day—early morning (grinding at the mill), mid-day (working in the field), and night (in bed)—thus suggesting that when Christ returns, it will be day in some places, but night in others, day and night, at the same time (Collett n.d., 277). This could not have reference to the destruction of Jerusalem, but must represent a "coming" of the Lord that will affect men globally.

Additionally, during Jerusalem's calamity, it was not a matter of some taken and some left—**all were taken!** More than a million Jews were slaughtered and thousands of others were taken into foreign slavery (Josephus, *Wars of the Jews* 6.9). Geldenhuys states that "not a single Jew was left alive in the city or its vicinity" (1960, 141).

Fifth, the Lord refers to a societal situation. The final day will be like the coming of a thief, who never warns or gives clues as to the time of his encroachment (vv. 42, 43). The Christian thus is cautioned to "watch," for in an hour "that ye think not the Son of man cometh" (v. 44).

Again, the point is: The time of Jesus' return cannot be anticipated. This clearly divorces the Lord's second coming from those "signs" associated with the fall of Jerusalem.

Conclusion

As we conclude, we feel compelled to emphasize again:

1. Those who view Matthew 24 as a thematic unit, pertaining only to end-of-time things, are wrong in their view of this context. This is the error of dispensational premillennialism.

2. Those who would merge 24:4-34 with 24:35-51, asserting that the entire chapter refers to the destruction of Jerusalem, are also mistaken in their concept of this chapter.

CHAPTER 5
The Preterist View Heresy

Note: The following editorial by Bill Reeves on this subject that he wrote in 1979 in an eight (8) part presentation for the Truth Magazine. He gave me permission to use it here just as he wrote it. Nothing has been added. It is presented in this venue just as he wrote it.

About a year ago Max King, of Warren, Ohio, came out with his new book, entitled *The Spirit of Prophecy*, advocating a Preterist-View of prophecy. This teaching has caused a mild furor among the liberal brethren (as respects institutionalism and centralization) wherever it has had a hearing. The following series of articles will review this novel doctrine, as set forth in a series of lectures by King before the Brookwood Way church of Christ, Mansfield, Ohio, in the summer of '70 (a taped recording of which I have), in several presentations which he and C. D. Beagle made before groups of liberal preachers last year ('71) (and also recorded), and in King's book. In this series I will use footnote 1 to refer to the recorded series in Mansfield, footnote 2 to the tape-recording of the discussions before several "preachers' meetings" last summer, and A- (plus a number) to refer to his book and page number.

The word "preterit" means past. I am told that he used "preterit" or "preterist" in his series at Brookwood Way; perhaps he did. However, it aptly describes his doctrine: *all prophecy is fulfilled and there is no event yet future from today referred to in the Scriptures.* So, there will be no future, physical resurrection of bodies from the grave, no coming of Christ in judgment, no future place called "heaven" to enter. *Everything is in the past*, as of A. D. 70, when Jerusalem was destroyed by the Romans!

After setting forth King's novel doctrine, by quoting from his speeches and writings, this series will discuss Paul's allegory of Gal. 4, which allegory King perverts beyond what the apostle Paul would recognize! Doing some additional allegorizing of his own, King takes his perversion of Paul's allegory and makes it the premise of his Preterist-View heresy. So much is his perversion of Paul's allegory essential to his view of prophecy that he has said: "That allegory of Paul, Gal. 4, is rich in giving us the key of the Bible, changing from the fleshly to the spiritual. It is the key passage because here we come from Ishmael to Isaac. And when are we going to come to Isaac? at the fall of this world (pointing to his chart and referring to the destruction of Jerusalem, A.D. 70--BHR) and bringing in the new." "This allegory of Paul, it's living--it's good!"

King affirms: "Throughout the brotherhood I have found a tremendous change to this view." Maybe his adjective is a little strong, but what false doctrine has ever wanted for adherents? It has already caused trouble near the area of my labors.

Following the treatment of the Galatians 4 allegory, I will take up some different aspects of King's doctrine and examine them. We will notice how he plays on words throughout his presentations, making subtle shifts from one word to another, leaving the impression that such and such passages are talking about what he is! I will give some examples of his misrepresentations of our positions. I will discuss some of the passages which he considers his big guns, and they will be spiked! We will read some of his pitiful explanations of texts so obviously against his heresy. There is so much to expose! As a friend remarked to me: "It would take a whole year to answer all the error in that book!" I have no intention of burdening this publication with an endless review of the innumerable errors of King's book, so, at the close of this series, if anyone would care to communicate with me on any given point in his teaching, I would be happy to offer any help that I can, from copious notes taken on more than 200 passages presented by him in his presentations.

Throughout the book King broadcasts a host of scripture-references, which impresses the unwary. I have just taken a random sample of ten pages and find on each one an average of fourteen passages cited! Yet, he runs silent on references when occasionally the consequences of his doctrine are pressed. For example, "Where does man go *today* when he experiences physical death?" A-179 On the next page he cites 1 Cor. 15:57, but he is committed to apply *that* text to the "victory" realized by A.D. 70! A-202 His impressive array of texts reminds us of the tactic of the Baptist debater in presenting a long list of texts on "faith," in support of his proposition of salvation by "faith only." It looks good, but what does it prove?

King is cautious as he addresses himself to the task of implanting his doctrine in the minds of his brethren. He is well aware of how foreign is his doctrine to the "traditional" view ("It may be a different concept than is traditional . . . ." A-204 Maybe, indeed!). Throughout the book such expressions as the following are employed: "there seems to be," "if this be the meaning" (referring to his own conclusion!), "it is only reasonable to assume," "this hardly seems reasonable" (Objecting to his opponent's position), "seems fairly obvious," "if this view is correct," "the thought or idea seems to be," "the N.T. seems to deal with," "quite likely," "it appears," "as intimated," "it seems to be dealing," "seems more agreeable," "may be intended," etc. Would King use such terms in debate with a Baptist preacher on the essentiality of baptism for the remission of sins? Now, can you imagine King's referring to a position purportedly taken by us and then saying to us, "Proof, please"? A-85 But of his own positions it suffices to speak thusly, "The author believes so." A-94 He must have proof, but we should content ourselves with his "think-so's."

King's doctrine, like all false doctrines (e.g., the Catholic doctrine of Purgatory, the "societies" of the denominations, the "sponsoring-church" of our erring brethren, etc.) must have a specially-created vocabulary, or lingo. He invents phrases and employs them as if they were obvious in the references cited. He speaks of Christ's "hidden divinity," A-108 "times of Christ," A-98 "raise up . . . to its rightful place" A-144 (in reference to "deliver up," 1 Cor.15:24), "undelivered kingdom . . . eternal or delivered kingdom," A-202 "resurrection of the saints into their own land," A-173 "full heritage in their new heaven and earth," A-215 etc.

Take from him his "King-size" convenience of special vocabulary and lingo, and his case becomes hopeless. So important is this necessity that he begins his book, giving his reasons for the *constant* use throughout the book of the terms "spiritual" and "literal." Monotonously he speaks of "spiritual" versus "literal," although he himself admits that these two terms are *not true opposites*! "The two methods of interpretation that will receive primary consideration are the 'literal' and the 'spiritual.' The 'literalists' object to making *literal* opposed to *spiritual* because in *true definition* (emphasis mine--bhr) literal does not necessarily imply material or non-material states. But the same problem exists with reference to the term 'figurative,' which is the true opposite of 'literal' . . . Thus the advocates of 'literalism,' (King does not say "the literal method"--bhr) do not want their *material* concepts represented by the term *literal*, and the advocates of the 'spiritual method' (King does not say "spiritualism," and so throughout his book he subtly switches terms--bhr) do not want their *non-material* concepts represented by the term *figurative*." A-1

The true opposite of "spiritual" is "material," and of "literal," "figurative." King admits it. Furthermore, he concedes: "It is not the writer's purpose, however, to...imply that material things are by nature opposed to spiritual things." A-8 But King is going to push his doctrine by consistently throughout the book making *literal* mean *material*, and *spiritual* mean non-material; and that, regardless! If one does not accept his "spiritual" interpretation, then by implication he is dwelling in the flesh and is materialistically-minded. King never finds "spiritual" opposite "literal" in the Scriptures, but after quoting texts that contrast "spirit" and "flesh," for example, he immediately reverts to "spiritual" versus "literal," and that for a purpose! This effort is designed to deny any *literal* resurrection, judgment-day, and a place called heaven to be entered at a time *future from today*!

King attaches to his chosen terms his own peculiar meanings and then plies the minds of his hearers and readers with them hoping by this bit of psychology to lead their thinking to his conclusions. He plays with words constantly throughout his speeches and book. (We will try to find space in these articles to cite a number of examples). He quotes texts using such terms as "world," "earth," "land," and "age," and runs them together to suit his purpose, ignoring the different Greek words from which they are taken. He likes the KJV of the Scriptures, when the English words lend themselves to his suggestions, but leaves it for Berry's Interlinear Greek N.T. (word-for-word translation) when that suits him. He indeed (and with admitted capability) has employed many devices of sophistication in the composition of his book.

In the next article we will quote him, to set forth a summary of what the Preterist-View of prophecy is all about, and then we will deal with his perversion of Paul's allegory. Galatians chapter 4.

The Preterist View Heresy (II)
XVII, 10 (11 Jan. 1973)

We continue our review of Max King's book, *The Spirit of Prophecy*. The title is taken from Rev. 19:10, "for the testimony of Jesus is the spirit of prophecy." This is typical of King's play on words. He needs some Scriptural approbation for his doctrine, and these words happen to come close to his "spiritual" interpretation of prophecy. He half-way admits ("While this may not be the purpose of this verse" A-2) that this verse is not touching on the *nature* of prophecy (i.e., whether prophecy is to be interpreted as "spiritual" or "literal," -- King's choice of words!), still within a few lines we find him slipping his ideas in: "it is only reasonable to assume that the *nature* or the spirit of prophecy..." (emphasis mine--bhr). This is typical of the handling of the Scriptures that the wary reader observes as he wades through King's book. He knows that the verse means that the testimony of Jesus is the life and soul of the prophecy (book of Revelation, for the Greek text says, "the prophecy"). But when his Preterist-View of prophecy, with a nature that is "spiritual" instead of "literal," needs a few Bible words to give it respectability, he finds some convenient ones in Rev. 19:10. How subservient have the Scriptures been made to the inventions of men!

Here are some quotes to set forth his doctrine: "...that the Jewish age came to a close on Pentecost day" is "another erroneous concept. This is assumed on the basis that Pentecost was the beginning of the Christian age. The error is in failing to see the overlapping period of these two ages or dispensations. Ishmael and Isaac co-existed in Abraham's house for a time before Ishmael was cast out. The Jewish age did not end until their city, temple and state fell under Roman invasion in A.D. 66-73." A-79 "Applying the last days to the *Christian* Age is a misapplication fostered by a misconception of such terms as 'this world' and 'the world to come.' While Pentecost, in a sense, was the beginning of the Christian dispensation, yet the New Testament writers often spoke of it as a world or age to come, because the Jewish age had not yet ended at the time of their writings. (The right of *primogeniture* belonged to Ishmael until he was cast out.) Therefore, statements such as 'this world' are interpreted as meaning this present material world rather than the Jewish Age, and the 'world to come' is interpreted as meaning what follows the end of this present material world rather than the new heaven and earth, or Christian age that followed the end of the Jewish age." A-79 "Because scholars have separated in time the fall of Jerusalem and the second coming of Christ, exegetical confusion in various passages of scripture is the inevitable result." A-81 "There is no time period between the fall of Judaism and the second coming of Christ." A-81

So, King affirms that the Jewish age did not end until A.D. 70. and that the Christian age did not begin until then; it was still "coming" until that date. He half-heartedly concedes that Pentecost *in a sense* was the beginning of the Christian dispensation (King, just which scripture teaches that?), but really it did not come until A.D. 70. Make up your mind, friend! Is A.D. 33 the beginning, or not? Your doctrine says "no," but "in a sense" it was. What confusion!

"When Paul wrote the allegory of Gal. 4, Ishmael had not yet been cast out. He was still in the household of Abraham, nudging Isaac, giving him a few short jabs now and then. Paul said to the Galatians, 'You hold on because the time of your redemption draweth nigh.'" A-2 "Keep in mind the over-riding of Judaism." A-2

King says that "Israel stuck right in that household until God threw him out! He had the inheritance, the first privileges, right up until the day that Jerusalem was destroyed." This is *King's* allegory! Sarah brought Ishmael into the picture, not God, and *she* cast him out, not God. God approved of the casting out because Ishmael never had any inheritance at all in God's promises to Abraham!

King builds heavily upon Romans 4:13, making "world" there refer to some perfect, complete state of things, once national Israel is destroyed in A. D. 70. "Inheriting the earth," Matt. 5:5, must refer to this same "world." (King runs similar expressions or words together according to his fancy). Judaism (which word he uses loosely, sometimes referring to the law, most of the time to national Israel) is referred to as the old heaven and earth, and the new heaven and earth is the supposed "perfect," "full inheritance," and "complete" something after A. D. 70! "The saints were waiting, not only for adulthood, but especially for their full manifestation as sons of God at the appearing of Christ in the fall of Judaism." A-234 "The fall of Judaism . . . was the coming of Christ in glory that closely followed his coming in suffering (1 Pet. 1:11), when all things written by the prophets were fulfilled (Luke 21:22; Acts 3:21). It corresponded to the perfection of the saints (1 Cor. 13:10) when they reached adulthood in Christ, receiving their adoption, redemption, and inheritance. The eternal kingdom was possessed (Heb. 12:28) and the new heaven and earth inherited (Matt. 5:5; Rev. 21:1,7). Out of the natural body (which received its death blow, Heb. 8:13) arose the spiritual body, wherein were manifested in glory, fully clothed with their house from heaven (2 Cor. 5:1-5). The earnest of the spirit (miraculous gifts) did not fail in power or purpose, bringing the *gift* of spiritual or heavenly inheritance to all the seed of Abraham (Acts 2:38,39; Gal. 3:28,29; 1 Pet. 1:4)." A-239

That last quote is a typical jumbling of texts together, with complete disregard for contexts, and a play on words, which things characterize King's fanciful doctrine.

On heaven King says: ". . . a growing, developing, relationship with God is the best definition of heaven I can think of at this time . . .Heaven is just joy and peace and right-living, right-thinking, right conduct . . . heaven is part of your life now, and when you die you live on and on and on . . . You'll never get any closer to heaven than that which you make in your own life." King, will a sinner get any closer to *hell* than that?

What about all those references in the Scriptures to a future end of all things, and of "comings?" They must be "allegorized" and "spiritualized" (God forbid that anything should be taken literally!) so as to be seen as Preterit, past, as of A.D. 70! King says, "I don't know what the destiny of this physical world is that we're living in."

Now to his "key" passage, Gal. 4:21-31. The *purpose* of Paul's allegory of Sarah and Hagar is presented in v. 21. This is *Paul's* purpose; King has a different one in mind! This allegory serves its inspired purpose when it is applied to the invalidness of the Law of Moses, now that the New Testament of Christ has been established. Any other use of this allegory is a perversion! Re-read, please, v. 21.

Abraham had two sons (v. 22). In the sense that Paul speaks of, of course this is true. In another sense it can be said that he had more than two (Gen. 25:1-6). Furthermore, in a very special sense it must be said that he had only one (22:2). But, respecting the circumstances of this allegory, he had two: Ishmael and Isaac.

In the allegory Hagar (the servant) represents the Law of Moses given on Mt. Sinai, and so the Old Testament, and Ishmael (born according to natural law) represents the Jews under the Law. On the other hand, Sarah (the freewoman) represents the Law of Christ, and so the New Covenant and Isaac (born miraculously and according to promise) represents Christians of all races. As Hagar and Ishmael were cast out, so was fleshly descendancy from Abraham of no merit in determining heirship. The "blessing of Abraham" and "promise of the Spirit through faith" (Gal. 3:14) was justification from our sins (v. 8). The Judaizers sought this justification by the law (5:4), and so, Paul by means of this allegory showed the Galatian brethren the consequences of desiring to be under the law: it was to be like Ishmael and Hagar; i.e., to be cast out! They were no part of God's promise to bless the seed of Abraham!

This allegory condemns premillennialism, that holds out a hope for national Israel, the Sabbatarians, the denominational practices that are based on the Old Testament (such as instrumental music in worship), and King's Preterist-View of prophecy. I call the reader's attention to the following list of facts recorded in Genesis:

(1) The call of Abraham and the triple promise that God made to him (in great nation, in land, in blessing all nations of earth) -- 12:1-7.

(2) Who would be Abraham's heir? Eliezer? No, says Jehovah, "but he that shall come forth out of thine own bowels shall be thine heir." -- 15:1-6. God's promises (12:1-7) did not depend upon human plans and arrangements.

(3) The birth of Ishmael, as a result of human plans according to natural law -- 16:1-16. Abraham was then 86 yrs. old. It was *not* the work of God! God's promises no more depended on Ishmael than upon Eliezer.

(4) God renewed his pact with Abraham. Abraham proposed that Ishmael might be the one by whom God's promises could be realized. Again God rejected human plans. God promised Abraham and Sarah a son, in spite of human impossibility due to the advanced age of the two. "I will establish my covenant with (Isaac)," the son of promise and according to *divine* plan -- 17:15,16,19-21.

(5) The birth of Isaac when Abraham was 100 years old; his weaning at the age of one to three years old (according to Jewish tradition); the mocking of Ishmael, and the casting out of Hagar and Ishmael from Abraham's house -- 21:1-12. The casting out was fully approved by God because the promised seed of Abraham would be called through the only heir, Isaac (v. 12). The Divine Plan from the beginning (chap. 12) depended solely upon God. Isaac was the only one ever in the plan of God to make Abraham a father of many nations (Gen. 22:2,12; Rom. 4:11-18; Heb. 11:17-19).

(6) The grand promise to Abraham fulfilled in Christ Jesus -- 22:18. Read Gal 3:14-18. Christ is the seed of Abraham by which all the world (Jew and Gentile) can be blessed with the salvation of their souls.

(7) From the beginning of the promises (chap. 12) Isaac was the heir in the purposes of God, and no other was (such as Eliezer and Ishmael). Even as respects the inheritance of material goods, Abraham's sole heir was Isaac (25:5,6). Even if Ishmael had not been cast out of the household, he still would not have inherited, even as Abraham's other sons (by concubines)

did not inherit anything. From beginning to end, Isaac was he only heir!

King is dead wrong in his claim that Ishmael had primogeniture until such time as he was cast out. He never had such a thing! He came on the scene by human wisdom (Sarah's), and left it the same way! He never was any part of God's purposes to bless mankind. Hagar and Ishmael typified the Law of Moses given at Sinai inasmuch as the Law was added 430 years after the promise of God was made to Abraham, and was taken away when the seed (Christ) came. See Gal. 3:17-19, 24, 25; 4:30. Sarah knew that Ishmael was not the heir in God's sight and plans, and cast him out that he might not so appear to others.

Paul did not tell the Galatians to "hang on" till A. D. 70, when they would really inherit something, and be completely manifested as the sons of God, etc. (per King's imagination), but that to desire to be justified by the Law of Moses (as the Judaizers did) was to desire to be under that which was cast out. They were *already* sons of the freewoman (and therefore justified in Christ--4:31; 5:1, 13; 2:4; Rom. 8:15; 2 Cor. 3:17). Their adoption as sons was *not* something to wait for as yet future (Gal. 4:17)! They had already passed from bondage to the adoption of sons. They were already complete in Christ (Col. 2:10).

King says: "Isaac was a grown man before he inherited . . . He did not receive the inheritance the day he was born . . . neither did the church receive its inheritance the day it had its beginning . . . One world ended (destruction of Jer., A. D. 70 -- bhr) and another one began . . . I stand there tonight because that's the meaning of the allegory." That's *King's* allegory; it is not found in Galatians 4!

The Preterist View Heresy (III)
XVII, 11 (18 Jan. 1973)

One of Max King's "big guns" is Rom.4:13. "According to Paul, a promise was given to Abraham that he and his seed would inherit a world." A-33 ". . . he did not look for inheritance in the Jewish world, but rather the Christian world . . . This truth is manifest in Heb.11:8-16." A-34 "This city he looked for, which hath foundations was the heavenly Jerusalem, Heb.12:22, or the Jerusalem which is above (Gal. 4:26). This is the new heaven and earth promised to Abraham and his seed, of which the Jewish world (old heaven and earth) was a forerunner. The New Testament saints, born of Abraham's spiritual seed, looked for this new world (2 Pet.

3:13), in anticipation of the time Ishmael would be cast out, or the old heaven and earth would pass away. The time was drawing near when the Hebrew letter was written. 'Now that which decayeth and waxeth old is ready to vanish away.' (Heb. 8:13)." A-35

To this King adds Matt. 5:17,18, making Jesus say that the "heaven and earth" of that passage refers to the passing away of Judaism in A.D. 70 at which time "all things would be accomplished." Also, the "heaven and earth" of Matt. 24:35 apply to the "Jewish world" (as he calls it for convenience sake--oh, how he plays with words!) to pass away in A. D. 70. He sees the word "world" in Rom 4:13, and so he gets "earth" out of Matt. Ch. 5 and Ch. 24, "land," "country," and "city" out of Heb. 11 and 12, and "world" out of Eph. 3:12 (KJV!), and runs them all together into his fanciful theory. Let's analyze these texts.

(1) Rom. 4:13. The Greek word here for "world" is *kosmos*. We do not read in Genesis of a promise stated in this style, but the context of Rom. 4 makes it clear that the reference is to his becoming the father of many nations in a spiritual sense. See especially vv. 16-18. See Gal. 3:29. The faith of the gospel is for all the world (Phil. 1:27; Mk. 16:15). Abraham, then, inherited the world as his spiritual children, for in his seed (Christ) all the world can be blessed, and the church is made up of all nations. Paul did not say that Abraham would inherit "a world." That's King's lingo. Abraham inherited the world as Jesus inherited the nations (Ps. 2:8; Heb. 1:2). Abraham was made a father of many nations in that he was the father of the faithful, of those with faith in Christ. They were spiritual progenitors. That's why Gal. 3:29 is so!

(2) Matt. 5:17,18. There is no "world" (kosmos) in this text. Jesus did not say that heaven and earth (Greek, GE) would pass away when all things were accomplished. King sees the word "earth," which is somewhat suggestive of "world," and away he runs with it! What does a context matter to him? Jesus is saying that his purpose in coming to the earth was not to destroy the law or the prophets, but to fulfill them. Furthermore, he says, until that is accomplished it would be easier for heaven and earth to pass away than for one jot or one tittle of the law or prophets to fall. See Lk. 16:17. Or, to put it another way, as long as heaven and earth stood, that law would be fulfilled without the least particle of it going unfulfilled. He came to fulfill it, and fulfill it he would, and heaven and earth would not pass away first! If the law was not fulfilled till A.D. 70, Christians were under it until then, and Paul says, "no" (Rom. 6:14).

(3) Matt. 24:35. Here Jesus speaks, not, as King does, of a "world" (kosmos), but of the same earth (GE) as in 5:18. The physical heaven and earth are temporary; they shall pass away (King's spiritualizing to the contrary. He says that he does not know "what the destiny of this physical world is that we're living in"), but Christ's declarations are *not* temporary, but are absolute of fulfillment, irrespective of time and temporal things. *That* is Christ's point, but King plays with the word "earth," and equates it with his "world" of Rom. 4:13.

(4) Matt. 5:5 is also cited by King and referred to his "Christian world" of A. D. 70. He says, "The residence of God's people today is in the new earth promised, which is just as spiritual as everything that belongs in it. Of this earth and this inheritance, Jesus spake in Matt. 5:5 . . ." A-26 Jesus is speaking of no such invention! The 37th Psalm (vv. 9, 11, 22, 29,34) shows that the expression "inherit the earth" means to benefit from its physical blessings. The beatitudes refer to a specific class of people and to what benefits they have because they *are* that class of people.

(5) Heb. 11:8-16. The Hebrew writer was no "A. D. 70 Advocate." He tells us to follow Abraham in seeking for a "city" (residence) which is *heavenly*. (King wished it said: "spiritual!") *Here* (on this earth and in this life) we do not have an "abiding city," or permanent residence. We seek after the one that is to come. (Heb. 13:14). It is in the "Father's house," Jn. 14:2. King equates the word "city" (of Heb. 11:10, 16) with "heavenly Jerusalem," which is his perfect state of things as of A. D. 70. King is the only authority for that! The Hebrew writer is contrasting a *heavenly* country with the *earthly* one in which Abraham, Isaac and Jacob lived as strangers and sojourners. One was on earth; the other in heaven. That's where Peter says that the eternal inheritance is reserved -- "in heaven" (1 Pet. 1:4).

(6) Heb. 12:22. "The tense of the verb *'are come'* shows that he was speaking of things that were transpiring at the time he wrote the Hebrew letter." "But ye are come . . . present tense! And we have the *new world* today." Brother King needs to check the Greek text; it is *not* present tense, but what is even worse for him the *perfect* tense! They had already arrived at that "city" (the heavenly Jerusalem) at the time the Hebrew writer wrote. "Are come" is not present tense; if present tense, it would read "are coming," and that is precisely what King advocates: that something was presently coming and would arrive in A. D. 70! The Hebrew writer used the perfect tense, as he did in v. 18, and tells the Hebrews that they had already arrived and were there. The perfect tense in

the Greek emphasizes action in the past with present consequences. The Hebrew Christians did not pertain to the Old Covenant, but they did (already) to the New! That's the point of the inspired writer. King plays with words and makes "are come" *are coming*, and hopes we will not see the difference. Paul made the brethren come to the "city," and King makes the "city" come (just a little later on) to the Hebrew brethren. *Berry's Interlinear*, as does the NASV, reads: "you have come," which is the clearest way to express the perfect tense in English.

Heb. 12:22 is present perfect tense, and, by contrast, Jn. 14:3; 2 Tim. 4:18; and 2 Pet. 1:11 are future. How King would like for the four texts all to be in the same tense!

(7) Gal. 4:26. The Jerusalem of this passage, as that of Heb. 12:2, are the same and refer to the New Covenant. Of course Christians had arrived, having arrived at the New Covenant of Christ. Of course perfection was there found (Heb. 10:1, 4). That's where they pertained. To go back to the Old Covenant would have been apostasy and perdition. That's the inspired writer's point. But King would like for Gal. 4:26 and Heb. 12:22 to say "new heavens and new earth," which phrase applies to the redeemed as viewed in heaven and in eternity, but not upon this earth. The New Testament views the saved as the kingdom of heaven now, on earth, and pertaining to the heavenly Jerusalem, and it also views the saved throughout eternity as the heavenly or eternal kingdom. King rejects this N.T. concept completely!

(8) 2 Pet. 3:13. Future tense, Brother King! The Hebrew Christians were already *arrived* at the heavenly Jerusalem City, but were looking forward to "new heavens and a new earth."

(9) Heb. 8:13. King says: "He nailed it to the cross to this extent: that he came to fulfill it and when he died upon the cross he did that and then Heb. 8:13; it took some forty years before the whole thing was completed." "The New Testament saints, born of Abraham's spiritual seed, looked for this new world (2 Pet. 3:13), in anticipation of the time Ishmael would be cast out, or the old heaven and earth would pass away. The time was drawing near when the Hebrew letter was written. (Heb. 8:13)." A-35 King cites Ps. 102:25-28, and says, " 'Yea, all of them shall wax old like a garment: 'does not this figure of speech sound familiar? See again Heb. 8:13; 'Now that which decayeth and waxeth old is ready to vanish away.' Could Paul and David be talking about the same event? The author

believes so" A-41 "(Heb. 8:13). The words 'ready to vanish away' are very significant in this passage, showing that the old dispensation continued several years after the cross. Its final end came with the fall of Jerusalem . . . and this event marked the passing of heaven and earth." A-184, 185 "This *natural body*, receiving its death blow at the cross and beginning then to wax old and decay (Heb. 8:13), became a nursery or seed-body for the germination, growth, and development of the spiritual body by means of the gospel. Thus, out of the decay of Judaism arose the spiritual body of Christianity, that became fully developed or resurrected by the end-time. Hence, this is the primary meaning of Paul's statement, 'It is sown a natural body; it is raised a spiritual body. There is a natural body and there is a spiritual body.'" A-200

The word "decayeth" (KJV of Heb. 8:13) is imperative to King's argument. He cannot use Berry here, or the ASV or NASV. They do not say "decay," and his fanciful theory needs a putrefying body for a period of time. But there is no decaying process of a dead body anywhere in the Greek word of this text, nor in the context. Notice the Greek text here: *to de palaioumenon kai geraskon*. Berry gives this literal word-for-word translation: "But that which grows old and aged." The ASV says: "But that which is becoming old and waxeth aged." The NASV reads: "But whatever is becoming obsolete and growing old." *Palaioumenon*, according to *Thayer's Greek Lexicon*, means, to declare a thing to be old and so about to be abrogated," and the second Greek word under consideration, *geraskon*, means "to fail from age, be obsolescent." The Hebrew writer does not say that the Old Covenant was becoming obsolete and growing old, but that *whatever* (neuter) is becoming obsolete and growing old is ready to disappear! That's his point; such is true of anything like that. It is a statement of general application. That's why the neuter is used: "that which," or "whatever." And, there's no *decaying* in the word!

Now, notice Ps. 102:25-27. There is no direct reference at all in Heb. 8:13 to this passage. There is a similar phrase there, and King jumps on it to make a play on words! The phrase "wax old" in Ps. 102:26, in the Septuagint (Greek version of the O.T.), is from the first of the two words noted above, meaning become old, or grow old. No "decaying" in Psa. 102 nor in Heb. 8! Even the KJV, in Psa. 102, does not say "decay" for the same word which appears in Heb. 8:13.

The Hebrew writer indicates that God considered the Old Covenant as obsolete in *Jeremiah's* time! When did God say that he would make a *new* covenant? Back in Jeremiah's time! What did God do to the first covenant when He said that? He made it old. What about anything old and obsolete? It is near to disappearing. This is what Heb. 8:13 is talking about! "When God announced a new covenant he proclaimed the insufficiency of the old, and the promise of a new covenant carried with it the promise of the abrogation of the old." (*Vincent's Word Studies in he N. T.*, p. 1135). The Hebrew brethren would be foolish to abandon the New Covenant for one done away! The Jews for six centuries knew, from Jer. 31:31ff, that the Old Covenant was in the aging process, and therefore would be abrogated in time. King gives the Law a "decaying" process six centuries too late!

The Preterist View Heresy (IV)
XVII, 12 (25 Jan 1973)

This is article four of several reviewing Max King's *Spirit of Prophecy*. He perverts the allegory of Paul, Gal. 4, doing some "allegorizing" of his own about "two sons in Abraham's household at the same time," and comes up with an "overlapping" of the "Jewish world" and the "Christian world." His constant play on words is imperative if he is to establish his Preterist-View doctrine. We now notice his "big gun," *mello*.

He cites Matt. 16:27; Acts 17:31; 2 Tim. 4:1; Heb. 10:27; and Rom. 8:18, and tell us that these texts in the Greek employ the word "*mello*" which means "about." For example, concerning Acts 17:31 he says: "Paul told the Athenians to repent and turn to Christ because he was going to judge the world. But when? How soon would that judgment day come? Many feel that there is nothing in the text itself to indicate time, whether near or afar, but to this we can hardly agree. Most Greek interlinears will furnish this reading: 'Because he set a day in which he is about to judge the habitable world in righteousness, by a man whom he appointed.' " "Paul said God was *about* (mello) to judge the world. This word 'mello,' where found in the present, active, indicative tense signifies, not only *intention* of purpose but also *nearness* of action, meaning at the point of, or ready to do what has been stated. Had Paul meant to teach a judgment of 2000 or more years future, he certainly would not have used mello in any tense, and especially in the present tense. Therefore the judgment of the habitable world (*oikoumene*) was about to take place in Paul's day and in view of other related scriptures we have every reason to believe Paul's choice of words conveyed the meaning intended by the Holy Spirit." A-157, 158

True to King's style, he stays with the KJV when it suits him, and runs to the Greek text when convenient. Berry uses the word "about" in the texts cited by King (about to come, about to judge, etc.). Now, King, cite Berry on 1 Cor. 15:24! We will cite it for you: "when he shall have given up the kingdom . . ." Yet King confidently says: "I challenge anyone to show that Christ is going to *give up* the kingdom." He knows that no well-known English version employs that precise phrase, "give up," in 1 Cor. 15:24, but he forgot about Berry, whom *he* cites when convenient!

Let's now quote Berry, in his dictionary, on mello: *"To be about to do, to be on the point of doing . . . the verb may often be adequately rendered by our auxiliaries, will, shall, must; to delay,* only Acts 22. 16. The participle is used absolutely: *to mellon, the future,* Lu. xiii. 9; *ta mellonta, things to come,* Ro. viii. 38." So, the KJV, the ASV, and the NASV simply say "shall," or "will" instead of "about to," in the texts cited by King.

Berry translates phrases built on *mello* in this fashion, at times: Luke 13:9, "hereafter;" 1 Cor. 3:22, "coming things;" and 1 Tim. 6:19, "for the future." How *near* is *mello*, King, in these passages?

Thayer defines the word thus, ". . . to be on the point of doing, or suffering something . . . to intend, have in mind, think to . . . of those things which will come to pass by fixed necessity or divine appointment . . . in general, of what is sure to happen."

King quotes authorities like all false teachers: *just that part that suits him!* We shall have occasion to notice more of such in later articles.

The word *mello* appears in the Greek text in Matt. 11:14, "And if ye are willing to receive it, this is Elijah, that is to come." (ASV). The Greek phrase says, literally, "this is Elijah, the about to come one." For four hundred years (Mal. 4:5) there was a coming one. Jesus said that John the Baptist was that one. As Thayer says of *mello*, "of those things which will come to pass by fixed necessity or divine appointment," so John the Baptist was destined to come. That's what *mello* means here! At the time of Jesus' speaking, John *already had come* (v. 18)! That "about to come" lasted four centuries!

Rom. 5:14 employs the word *mello*, and *Berry's Interlinear* reads: "who is a figure of the coming one." The KJV reads: "him that was to come." The ASV and the NASV read the same. Actually, "was" is not in the Greek phrase per se, but is properly supplied by the context (see especially the next verse), because the point is that Adam was a type of Christ *in his first coming to die for man*! Christ was "about" to come for millenniums -- ever since the time of Adam! King would love for every *mello* passage to indicate something "about" to be in the near *future*! But when Paul wrote Rom. 5:14, the "about to come one" *already had come*! So King's play on words fails again!

So desperate is King for something "about to be" that he takes up the notion of "two comings of Elias." A-162 According to this fancy, John the Baptist was the first one, and the "first born ones or remnant of Israel were the messengers that prepared the way for Christ's second coming" A-162 in the destruction of Jerusalem, and were the second of the two Eliases. King bases this on Matt. 17:10-13, affirming that since "come" is present tense, and "shall restore" is future, that there was another Elias to come, future from then, and that the word of Preparation for Christ's coming in the destruction of Jerusalem, on the part of the saints, was the fulfillment of the second Elias to come!

Verse 11 is an abstract statement on the part of Christ showing that Elijah's coming precedes in time the coming of the Messiah. As for actual fact, Christ makes it crystal-clear in v. 12 that that Elijah had already come in the person of John the Baptist! John's work of "restoring all things" is set forth in Mal. 4:6 and Luke 1:17, and that is, in a word, his preaching of repentance (Matt. 3:1-12). So, the "two Elijahs" is another invention of false teachers desperate for proof.

King has a section on the two Adams. A-212ff Here he confuses or runs together (in his constant play on words) Rom. 5:14 and 1 Cor. 15:22. They are not of the same context, but what matters that to King who is most interested in words? Rom. 5:14 speaks of spiritual death and life, while 1 Cor. 15 of physical. King says, after quoting 1 Cor. 15:22, "But the question is; when did the second Adam make all in him alive? According to Paul, it was at the resurrection or the coming of Christ, when the natural body was raised a spiritual body. But is this still future? The writer thinks not, for Paul said in his Roman letter (60 A.D.) it was 'at the point' of happening then. Concerning Adam, Paul said, 'who is a figure of him that was to come,' (Rom. 5:14). The literal translation here is; 'who is a figure of the coming (one).'" A-213

Now let's answer King's question: If your question is based on 1 Cor.

15:22, the answer is that He has not done it yet! Paul *did not say* in 1 Cor. 15:22 that Christ was "at the point" of doing something. King ran back to Rom. 5:14 for his *mello*, and hoped that his readers would not catch him at it! But, if his question is based on Rom. 5:14, the answer is that He did it when he died on the cross, thus making justification possible. Friends, read the verses which follow Rom. 5:14, noting especially v. 18, and in chap. 6 vv. 11, 13, 18, 22. That all happened well before A. D. 70. It had already happened in A.D. 60, if that is when Paul wrote Romans. King presses his limited application of the word *mello* and tries to get Christ coming in A. D. 70 to do what Paul said He was the coming one to do: justify us sinners! If Paul meant that Christ had not come quite yet, then sinners were not quite yet justified until A. D. 70! What a doctrine!

On page 213 in his book, King refers to a good article in *Bible Herald*, Vol 18, No. 3 (commenting on Rom. 5:14 -- bhr). He says that the writer of that article "completely misses the point." The writer *does not*; but King is the one who not only completely misses the point, but misrepresents the writer at the same time! King very subtly slips in his "about-phrase" and says, "Paul did not say Christ was about to come in Adam's day . . ." Of course Paul did not, and no one said that he did say it! King is misrepresenting as so often he does when he refers to his opponents' positions. The writer in *Bible Herald* was saying what Paul *did say*, and that is that Adam was a type of one who was coming from the time of Adam until He finally did come, to die on the cross and make justification possible. That was well before A.D. 60! The "nearness" of fulfillment is no point of Paul's. Paul's point was that Christ was the anti-type of Adam, and as such was the coming one, or about to be one, in order to give life for death. *When* He came is determined by *when* he gave that life! V. 18, that "one act of righteousness" refers to the cross of A.D. 33! King ignores the context of Rom. 5 and 6, and jumbles it with that of 1 Cor. 15, to make out a case for his fanciful invention of one "world" rising up out of another one at A. D. 70.

The Preterist View Heresy (V)
XVII, 13 (Feb 1973)

In this article we take up 2 Peter 3:1-13, and elements. So obviously is this passage against King's Preterist-View that he labors hard to "explain it away," as he utilizes his favorite devices: ignoring of contexts, and running different ones together as if they applied to the same thing, play on words, and misuse of authoritative works.

When asked at Mansfield what he did with his Preterist-View in the light of 1 Pet. 3:10, he replied: "I apply it to this passage all the way, word for word, absolutely! . . . Everything to be on fire, yes! When he came in his personal ministry he lit the fire." (referring to Lk. 12:49 -- bhr). Lk. 12:49 represents an entirely different context. But, on 2 Pet. 3 he surrenders his "spiritualized" and "allegorized" exegesis by saying, "Yes, it has a secondary application. I have every reason to believe that some day this physical heaven and earth will melt away . . . because it is a type of the heaven and earth (the kingdom as of A. D. 70 -- bhr) that he said he would create." King has "every reason" but he does not name any and he gives no Scripture reference, because he has none. His so-called "secondary application" is an assertion without proof. In my second article I quoted him as saying, "I don't know what the destiny of this physical world is that we're living in." Some quotes from him now will show that he "spiritualizes" 2 Peter 3:1-13, but leaves the door open for escape by means of an invented "secondary application."

He makes the "world" of 2 Pet. 3:6 mean "people or age," and the "heavens . . . and the earth" of v. 7 mean the "Jewish world." He says, "How did the Jewish world burn with fire? Don't get back in the flesh; stay in the spirit! Let's see the spiritual significance of these fleshly symbols." King "spiritualizes" a literal passage and calls you fleshly if you do not accept his "allegorizing." This he does throughout his book. That is why he insists on *his* opposites: spiritual versus literal. It is for effect. See my first article.

"Thus, the world reserved unto fire against the day of judgment and perdition of ungodly men (2 Pet. 3:7) was the Jewish world . . . Fiery judgment was going to fall on Judaism. Jesus said, 'I am come to send fire on the earth; and what will I, if it be already kindled' (Luke 12:49). The fire of 2 Pet. 3:10 is no more literal than the fire of Luke 12:49. (Why, the fire of Lk. 12:49 is not literal at all! There's no comparison! -- bhr) Other passages involving symbolic fire in the destruction of Judaism are: Matt. 3:12; 13:40, 42; and 2 Thes. 1:8." A-131

In the previous quote we see King at his old trick of running distinct contexts together. He wants "fire" symbolic in 2 Pet. 3, as it is in an entirely different context, Lk. 12:49. But the fire of 2 Pet. 3 is just as literal as the water of vv. 5, 6! We see King playing with words, as he slips in his "Jewish world," which is nowhere to be found in 2 Pet. 3:1-13. Peter is speaking of the literal, physical heavens and earth in vv. 7, 10, just as he is back in v. 5. King sees the word "world" (*kosmos*) in v. 6, and then tries to make the heavens and the earth (*ge*) a "world," and finally the "new heavens and a new earth" (*ge*), v. 13, another "world," too. On page 130 he affirms: ". . . we find *three* worlds in 2 Pet. 3," and goes on to identify them as the world that perished in the days of the flood, the "Jewish world," and the third one which was that perfect, complete something that followed "after Judaism fell." But King can find "world (*kosmos*) only once in 2 Pet. 3!

Let us see what Peter actually did say: (1) Ungodly men, who walked in their lusts (identified by this passage, by 2 Pet. 2:1ff; Jude, and 1 John, in particular, as the Gnostics), mocked the fact of Christ's coming in a "day of judgment and destruction of ungodly men," vv.1-7. (2) Their claim of uniformitarianism (v.4) was given the lie by the fact of the Noachian flood. God's word brought a literal, physical heaven and earth into existence. Out of chaos He brought an ordered arrangement. That ordered world (*kosmos*), v. 6, perished in the flood. A cataclysm destroyed that existing order of life on the earth, including the death of living creatures and the change of the earth's topography, leaving a new surface and a remnant of righteous people. It was a world-wide judgment! (3) The heavens that *now* are and the earth represent the order of things since the flood, and are just as real and literal as the antediluvian order. These are reserved by the same Word of God for a cataclysm of *fire*, and this fire is just as literal as that water! (4) Three things are mentioned in connection with the "day of the Lord," v. 10: (a) the heavens shall pass away with a great noise, (b) the elements shall be dissolved with fervent heat, and (c) the earth and the works that are therein shall be burned up.

Now, look at King's "thought for the literalists." A-186 "Why are the elements ascribed to the 'heavens' rather than the 'earth?' Peter said, '. . . wherein the heavens being on fire shall be dissolved and the elements shall melt with fervent heat.' (2 Pet. 3:12). It would seem more natural to speak of the 'elements' of the earth rather than of the heavens, if the material world were the subject." A-186,187 Again King engages in word-trickery! Peter did *not* ascribe the elements of the heavens, as distinct from the earth. Peter said nothing about the "elements of heaven." That's King's insinuation. See again, v. 10, the three things mentioned there. The expressions "dissolved with fervent heat," "burned up," "being on fire," and "melt with fervent heat," are used interchangeably in reference to the heavens, elements and earth.

King desperately needs some word to play on in order to get people's minds off of a literal, fiery destruction of the material universe, and onto the destruction of Jerusalem, and for this he uses "elements." Listen to him: "The word element in the scriptures means 'the rudimentary principles of religion . . . the elementary principles of the O.T., as a revelation from God, Heb. 5:12, R.V.' This same word is found in Gal. 4:3,9 where it is used in reference to the rudimentary principles of the Jewish system. Since law or government is involved in the meaning of heaven, it follows that the rudiments or elements of Judaism properly belong to the region of heaven. These were the elements that would melt with fervent heat, fire being a symbol of destruction." A-187 "Does 'elements' of the 'world' in Gal. 4:3 refer to the literal heavens and earth? None would dare so affirm. Could it not have the same application in 2 Pet. 3:10? It is also found in Gal. 4:9; Col. 2:8, 10. Yes, this was the world Christ was coming to destroy." A-42

King says that "the word element in the scriptures means . . ." King, does it mean that in *every* scripture? Is that the *only* meaning of the word? *You know better*!! Because you quote *part* of what Vine says and purposely omit the part against you. I shall quote *all* of what Vine says on the meaning of the word in the N.T.: "In the N.T. it is used of (a) the substance of the material world, 2 Pet. 3:10, 12 (King conveniently omitted this! -- bhr); (b) the delusive speculations of Gentile cults (King mentions only Judaism! -- bhr) and of Jewish theories, treated as elementary principles, 'the rudiments of the world, 'Col. 2:8, spoken of as 'philosophy and vain deceit;' these were presented as superior to faith in Christ; at Colossae the worship of angels, mentioned in ver. 18, is explicable by the supposition, held by both Jews *and Gentiles* (emphasis mine -- bhr) in that district, that the constellations were either themselves animated heavenly beings, or were governed by them; (c) the rudimentary principles of religion, Jewish or Gentiles (King mentions nothing about Gentiles in defining "elements," -- bhr), also described as the 'rudiments of the world,' Col. 2:20, and as 'weak and beggarly rudiments,' Gal. 4:3, 9, R.V., constituting a yoke of bondage; (d) the elementary principles (the A.B.C.) of the O.T., as a revelation from God, Heb. 5:12, R.V., 'rudiment,' lit., 'the rudiments of the beginning of the oracles of God,' such as are taught to spiritual babes." So, the reader can see how King deceitfully uses authoritative works on Greek words! The words which suit his theory he employs and conveniently leaves out all others!

Vincent, in his *Word Studies in the N.T.,* p. 336, 337, tells us that the Greek word for "elements" is applied "to four elements--fire, air, earth, water; and in later times to the planets and signs of the zodiac. It is used in an ethical sense in other passages; as in Gal. 4:3, 'elements or rudiments of the world.' Also of elementary teaching, such as the law. which was fitted for an earlier stage in the world's history; and of the first principles of religious knowledge among men. In Col. 2:8, of formal ordinances. Compare Heb. 5:12." Also, commenting on 2 Pet. 3:11, he says, "The world and all herein is essentially transitory." Commenting on v. 12, "melt," he says, "Literal. Stronger than the word in vv. 10, 11. Not only the *resolving*, but the *wasting away* of nature."

Thayer, in his lexicon, p. 589, says on this Greek word, as used in 2 Pet. 3:10, "the elements from which all things have come, the material causes of the universe." He includes Heb. 5:12; Gal. 4:3, 9, and Col. 2:8, 20 under his fourth definition: "the elements, rudiments, primary and fundamental principles (cf. our 'alphabet' or 'abc') of any art, science, or discipline." On Gal. 4:3, 9 he adds that these "elements" refer to "ceremonial precepts common alike to the worship of Jews *and of Gentiles* (emphasis mine -- bhr)." So, Vine, Vincent, and Thayer all say the same thing about "elements," as used in 2 Pet. 3, and not a one agrees with King. King takes one specific definition and applies it at will. This is his "long suit," throughout the book. Truth is not served by such tactics!

Lastly we notice one more play on words as respects King's teaching on 2 Pet. 3. Commenting on v. 10, "the earth and the works that are therein shall be burned up," he says, "The works that were to perish or be destroyed in the fiery judgment of that world were the works of the law." A-187 He had just quoted Gal. 2:16, because there Paul refers to the "works of the law." Of course there is no contextual connection, but so what? (to King, that is!) Peter said nothing about works of the law of Moses; he said the *earth* and the works in *it*!

There's the Preterist-View for you: when the Romans burned Jerusalem, 2 Peter 3 was fulfilled! *If you think that is bad, wait until you see his treatment of 1 Cor. 15, which we take up in the next article.*

The Preterist View Heresy (VI)
XVII, 14 (8 Feb 1973)

The Preterist-View of prophecy denies that there will be a future, bodily resurrection of the dead from the graves! King, therefore, runs right into

Realized Eschatology

the face of such passages as Jn. 5:28,29 and 1 Cor. 15, but he has the special "tools" of an A. D. 70 Advocate to "explain away" the obvious import of these and other related passages.

The *context* of 1 Cor. 15:12-58 has to do with the *literal* dead being raised, if Christ was *literally* raised from the *literal* dead (and even King admits that Christ was)! But the Preterist-View doctrine makes the discussion of our resurrection one from a *figurative* death (the dead and decayed "body" of Judaism). But, on the other hand, King (wanting to have his cake and eat it, too) invents his "secondary application" when he is in a tight and needs some Scripture to refer to what happens to us when we die. He then uses some verses from 1 Cor. 15 in his "secondary application." If we could convince ourselves that God has favored King with such liberty with the Scriptures, we could more easily be taken in by his fanciful doctrine!

To Christ, as Savior and Mediator, all authority in heaven and on earth was given (Matt. 28:18). As such Christ is now reigning and will, Paul says, "till he hath put all his enemies under his feet. The last enemy that shall be abolished is death." This "death" is just as literal as "dead" in v. 20. At such time, Paul says, Christ "will deliver up the kingdom to God." His *mediatorial* reign shall have ended. Of course, the reign of Christ and God in our hearts will never end, if we are faithful unto death, and are saved unto that heavenly kingdom, and have entrance into that eternal kingdom (1 Tim. 4:18; 2 Pet. 1:11). That will be when He comes the "second time," not as Mediator and Savior, but as Judge (Heb. 9:28; Acts 17:31).

But King must deny that at some date future from now Christ will deliver up the kingdom to God. He had to "deliver it up" back in A. D. 70! So, he must deny the obvious meaning of "deliver up," and give it a forced interpretation. Listen to him: On the word "till" he says: it means "when he *really* begins to reign in power; not a cessation of activity by a gathering up to a state of absolute power and perfection." "The word 'till' does not denote cessation of reign, but rather points to a time and an event that will be the zenith of his reign." A-144 He does not tell us where he gets this "zenith" business! He issues the following challenge: "I challenge anyone to show that Christ is going to give up (his chosen phrase -- bhr) the kingdom! He'll have it for ever and for ever and for ever!" Well, Brother King, we will be glad to accommodate you, by using a version you yourself turn to when the wording in the KJV does not suit your play on words: *Berry's Interlinear*. It reads, "when he shall have given up the kingdom." (P. 465). Of course Christ shall reign forever, and has an everlasting kingdom, but He will not reign forever as Mediator, with all authority given to Him. King, do you believe that time will continue forever, time as we know it? All authority was given to Christ for His mediatorial reign, and when that phase of His reigning is terminated, that authority shall be returned, and that is what the apostle Paul is saying in 1 Cor. 15. That people, saved and mediated by Christ, will be saved forever, and in that sense the kingdom is spoken of as eternal. That phase of the kingdom is yet ahead.

Let us look at Thayer's definition of the Greek word translated "deliver up:" "to give over into (one's) power, or use" (p. 481). The same Greek word (*paradidomi*) is found in John 19:30, and is translated in the KJV (of all places!) "give up." So, to "deliver up" is the very same idea as "give up," and King is challenging anyone to show the very thing that the apostle Paul declares! We simply turn over to Paul this play-on-word artist.

Now, since he likes challenges so well, we issue him one: Show us a version or Greek authority that translates paradidomi (deliver up) as "raise up or restore to rightful place." A-144 What a definition! And King has the audacity to issue challenges on definitions after such a wild one as that! He must think mighty highly of himself to expect people to accept his verbal inventions on no higher authority than his "ipse dixit."

King conveniently divides 1 Cor. 15 into sections. See pages 199-201. He says that vv. 1-20 are "given to the bodily resurrection of Christ himself." Note the phrase, "bodily resurrection." He uses this in reference to *Christ's* resurrection, but will not use it in reference to any one else's. Elsewhere he refers to the "traditional resurrection doctrine" A-211 as advocating a "fleshly resurrection," A-217 in distinction to his "spiritual resurrection." "The resurrection is spiritual and not fleshly." A-222 Repeatedly he contrasts "the fleshly view" A-225 with the "spiritual view." A-197 He speaks of the "literal body view" A-192 as opposed to the "spiritual body view." A-195 This special phraseology is used for effect! If one takes anything *literal*, he is *fleshly*, according to King! We believe in a *bodily resurrection*, but King insists on representing us as believing in a *fleshly* one. He believes in the bodily resurrection of Christ, but will not represent us as believing in a bodily resurrection of the dead, sometime future from now. According to King, ours is a fleshly view, a literal view, the traditional view!

Then, doing a switch on us, he gets off of the bodily resurrection and from

v. 21 to v. 58 he gets on his so-called "spiritual resurrection," while the apostle Paul stays on the *same subject*, vv. 12-58, and that is, the physical, bodily resurrection of the dead! On King's sections from v. 21 to v. 58, he uses his own invention of "primary resurrection" and "secondary resurrection," applying these sections primarily to "the rise of the Christian system itself" out of Judaism, once Jerusalem was destroyed, and secondarily to what happens to a man at death. "The natural body that was sown (verse 44) answers to the fleshly or carnal system of Judaism . . . from which came the spiritual body . . . . Judaism answers to the field or the world in which the good seed was sown (Matt. 13:37, 38). This *natural* body, receiving its death blow at the cross and beginning then to wax old and decay (Heb. 8:13), became a nursery or seed-body for the germination, growth, and development of the spiritual body by means of the gospel. Thus, out of the decay of Judaism arose the spiritual body of Christianity that became fully developed or resurrected by the end-time. Hence, this is the primary meaning of Paul's statement, 'It is sown a natural body; it is raised a spiritual body. There is a natural body and there is a spiritual body.'" A-200 So, that's how King man-handles 1 Cor. 15:21-58, while Paul sticks with his subject of a *bodily* resurrection, just like Christ's!

King denies that the "graves" of Jn. 5:28, 29 are literal. A-219 He makes this passage deal "with spiritual, not physical death." A-219 ". . . the end of Judaism . . . is the resurrection of John 5:28, 29." A-220 Before the Preachers' Meeting he said, "Yes, I believe Jesus arose physically from the dead," but of us he says, "personally, I don't hold to the view that there is a physical resurrection." "A physical resurrection, however, is denied." A-204

Well, after all of King's misrepresentation of our position, and all of his play on words, Jesus still is on record as saying, ". . . all that are in the tombs shall hear his voice, and shall come forth," and Paul, also, saying, "It is sown . . . it is raised." That which will be raised a spiritual body is the same as that which was sown. Of course we do not believe that a fleshly body will come from the grave, but that a spiritual body will, and will be the resurrection of that very body which was buried. 1 Cor. 15 describes the body in the grave as that which was "first," "natural," "terrestrial," "corruptible," "weak," "earthly," "flesh and blood," and "mortal," and declares that it will be resurrected a spiritual *body*. This is what King denies that the passage teaches. No wonder King does not believe in a bodily resurrection and will not properly represent us as so believing. He hopes by tying "fleshly" onto us we will be "scared" into his Preterist-View heresy!

He denies that Phil. 3:21 is yet to be fulfilled. According to him it does not refer to the physical body at all! "Why did he use the plural 'our' and the singular 'body,' if he were talking about a general resurrection of individual dead bodies?" A-194 "The redemption of *our body* (not bodies) in Romans 8:23 is equated with *our vile body* (not bodies) in Phil. 3:21, and corresponds to the redemption of the *purchased possession* or church in Eph. 1:14." A-194

King, by his forced interpretation of Rom. 8:23 and Phil. 3:21, gets himself into many difficulties. If the singular word "body" refers to the church as a spiritual body, then he has the church "vile," and has Paul referring to "our" church! But Paul in Rom. 8:18-25 contrasts the suffering in the *physical* body with the glory of the physical body once it is redeemed. In saying "our body," he uses a figure of speech which we call a "synecdoche," wherein the part is put for the whole (as fifty sails, for fifty ships). King wants to play on the fact that the word "body" is singular. Let him try his little play on 4:23, "your spirit" (did all the Philippians have but one spirit?); on 1 Thess. 5:23, "your spirit and soul and body" (did they have but one of each? or, if the "body" is the church, what is the "spirit" and the "soul?"); on Heb. 10:22, "our hearts" (plural), but "our body washed with pure water" (is the *church* baptized, King, or are individual *bodies* baptized? The Greek text says "body," not "bodies;" therefore, "body" as in the ASV and NASV).

In Phil. 3:21 the Greek text says, as the ASV renders it, "the body of our humiliation," or as the NASV, "the body of our humble state," and not "our vile body." Paul is contrasting v. 20 with v. 21. Whereas the enemies of the cross had only earthly citizenship, a glory pertaining to appetites of the belly, and an end characterized by perdition, Christians have a heavenly citizenship, a promise some day of the glorified body like Christ's for the physical body which in this life is subjected to humiliation, and an end characterized by salvation. Paul uses the singular, "body," just as he uses the singular, "spirit," in 4:23, etc. The one body is characteristic of each, individual one, and therefore the one is put for the many. This is common in the Scriptures. Note 1 Jn. 3:19-21, "our heart." But King knew this when he perverted Rom. 8:23 and Phil. 3:21. He has a theory to defend!

The Preterist View Heresy (VII)
XVII, 15 (15 Feb. 1973)

King versus Jesus, on Matt. 22:23-33. King, like the Sadducees of old, denies "a general resurrection of individual dead bodies." A-194 No wonder, then, that this passage gives him trouble. But, give King credit: he does meet it head on in his book, although he employs his customary sophistry to set aside its obvious import.

He blames the Pharisees' "fleshly concepts" for the Sadducees' unbelief. The Sadducees' "rejection of the resurrection was due largely to the fleshly concepts taught and believed in that day." A.217 Where did you learn that, King? Made it up, didn't you? Paul was a Pharisee! (Acts 23:6c, 8a, "I am a Pharisee, a son of Pharisees; touching the hope and resurrection of the dead I am called in question . . . For the Sadducees say that there is no resurrection, neither angel, nor spirit.")

"They reasoned that if the fleshly body were going to be resurrected in the last day . . . " A-217 Yes, the *fleshly* body, will be resurrected in the last day, but it will not be raised a *fleshly* body (1 Cor. 15:44). King very astutely misrepresents us repeatedly by referring to a "fleshly resurrection," rather than to a bodily resurrection. He knows there is a difference.

"But Jesus informed them that their problem existed in their ignorance of the nature of the resurrection." A-217 Note how subtly King inserts the word "nature" into the discussion. Ah, but he is subtle! No, King, the Sadducees did not deny the *nature* of the resurrection; they denied the *fact* of it! Read v. 23, and Acts 23:8, again, and notice also 26:8, 23. Those Sadducees affirmed: "there is no resurrection," just exactly like King affirms: there is no "general resurrection of individual dead bodies." King tries to slip the word "nature" into the discussion and pin Sadduceeism on us!

King speaks of the Sadducees' first error being that of not knowing the Scriptures, and their second one, that of not knowing the power of God. He is wrong again; they had but one error in this context: they denied the fact of the resurrection! Jesus says that in so denying it they showed both their ignorance of the Scriptures and the *power* of God. I emphasize "power" to alert the readers of King's book to the smoothness and subtlety of deceit he employs throughout it, for concluding matters, he says, "Thus, the failure of the Sadducees to know their scriptures and the promise (emphasis mine -- bhr) of God . . ." A-218 See how he switches terms in order to condition his readers' minds to his position? (He had just above written about the resurrection being for fulfilling to Abraham and to his seed the *promise* of a new heaven and earth, meaning his A.D. 70 doctrine).

It would take a book to expose the twisting and perverting of all the Scriptures which King has set forth in *The Spirit of Prophecy*. These few articles can take up only some samples of this play-on-words artist!

How King is hurting on Luke 20:27-40! Let us look at his pitiful attempt to "explain it away." Jesus in this passage talks about "this world" (aion, age) and "that world," and King's Preterist-View doctrine has to give such expressions a constant application: namely, the "Jewish world" and the "Christian world" (as of A.D. 70!). But Jesus is talking about life now on earth, and life in heaven after this life is no more, because he talks about a time when people marry, and a time when they will no more be doing so. If Jesus is talking about what *King* is, then since A.D. 70 there should have been no more marriage (and how could we possibly have gotten from A.D. 70 until now without marriage!) King knows this, and we now look at his perversion of Rom. 14:17, designed to help him out of his predicament.

He writes: "The statement that those in the world to come would neither marry nor be given in marriage is not, as it would appear on the surface, a denial of marriage or physical life in the Christian age. Rather, it has the meaning of Paul's statement that the kingdom of God is not meat and drink, but righteousness and peace, and joy in the Holy Ghost (Rom. 14:17). Jesus was not teaching that the citizens of the world to come 'do not marry' any more than Paul taught that citizens of the kingdom do not eat or drink. The point being debated is the nature of the world that was to come. The 'children of this world' (Jewish) were constituted as such by physical birth, being the fleshly seed of Abraham. Thus, the citizens of 'this world' were propagated by marriage or fleshly procreation. But such would not be true in the world to come (the Christian age). Jesus said those who would be worthy to obtain that world and the resurrection from the dead, would not do so by physical means or methods. It was not the kind of world that could be entered by flesh and blood (1 Cor. 15:50) . . . 'Neither can they die any more' because they are the 'children of the resurrection,' refers to the spiritual state of redeemed man, and not his physical state." A-237, 238

King can crowd more error, sophistry and perversion into one paragraph than anyone I have ever known! Let us note some of these:

(1) (Denying marriage or physical life in the Christian age). Of course what Jesus said is no such denial, for the simple reason that Jesus was not talking about the "Christian age." Jesus *does* deny that there will be marrying in the world to come. Since marriage is not denied us *now*, "that world" is not *now*! How King is hedging, here!

(2) (Citizens of the kingdom do not eat or drink). Rom. 14:17 has nothing in the world to do with the subject of Lk. 20:27-40. Jesus is talking about the world to *follow* the one we are living in now, and Paul is talking about our conduct as citizens of the kingdom *now*. What we eat and drink, or do not eat and drink, is not the basis of our conduct in the church, Paul says, in a context dealing with matters of indifference. But, incidentally, look what King has done: cited a text concerning conduct in the kingdom *before* A.D. 70! King, if he has a parallel at all, will have to affirm that Paul says, "for the kingdom of God *will not be* (after A.D. 70) eating and drinking, but righteousness . . ."

(3) (The point being debated is the nature of the world to come). This is King's desperate invention. As he did in handling Matt. 22, here he slips in the idea of "nature." *This is not Christ's point!* Christ is *not* talking about *how to get into* the world to come: whether by literal marriage or not! That's ridiculous, and King knows that he is perverting this context. Just which words of Jesus, King, do you cite to show that Jesus was talking about proper means or methods of attaining to that world? Jesus spoke of what people would *not be doing* once they did attain to it: they would not be marrying, giving in marriage, nor dying (*present tense* in the Greek text, which indicates continual, habitual action). King makes Jesus say that N.T. saints, of before A.D. 70, would not be able to get into King's complete and perfect something, coming when Jerusalem would be destroyed, by means of the marriage act!

(4) ("Neither can they die any more" does not refer to physical death). King expects us to accept this forced conclusion, in spite of the context of Luke 20:27-40. He slips in some texts dealing with spiritual death, and hopes we will not detect his tactics, his switching of terms! Well, the simple truth of the matter is that (a) the Sadducees, "they that say there is no resurrection," *period*! came to Jesus and propounded a case in which seven men *died physically*. Do you see that, King? Of course you do. (b)

Then the woman died, also; and that physically! (c) Jesus claimed that in the resurrection they do not do that anymore, King. They do not *die!* *physically!* Jesus said, they *cannot*. Why? Because they are like the angels, who do not die.

King represents us as "waiting for some miracle of spiritual renewal or transformation to take place in physical death," A-238 and in doing so, *misrepresents* us! Let us ask: King, is *that* the way you used to express it when for years you taught on the resurrection what we teach now? Before you left the truth, did you preach it like *that*? In those terms? For your benefit I will tell you what we are waiting for: we are waiting for the Lord Jesus Christ from heaven, who shall *fashion anew* (Greek, changing what is outward and shifting -- Vincent, p. 889; change the figure of -- Thayer, p. 406) the body of our humiliation, that it may be conformed to the body of His glory (Phil. 3:20, 21). We do not expect this at the moment of each one's death, for at death we sleep in Jesus and rest, but when he comes from heaven (1 Thess. 1:10; 4:16, 17; Heb. 9:28; 1 Cor. 15:20-23). The next time you write a book, brother, at least represent us correctly, regardless of what you teach!

"To put the new heaven and earth in contrast with this material world, making it essential for all material elements of creation to be destroyed before the new world can be created, misses the whole scheme of redemption, as well as the very nature of it. The world that failed to accomplish redemption, becoming a 'ministration of death' was the one the new heaven and earth followed, bringing a 'ministration of life and righteousness.' Any careful student of the Bible should be able readily to identify these two worlds and pinpoint the ending of the one and the beginning of the other." A-239

The new heavens and new earth *will* follow the dissolution of the elements of the material creation; Peter says so in the third chapter of the second book. Such does *not* miss the "whole scheme of redemption." King's Preterist-View is the culprit, because it makes a "ministration of death" (Judaism, as he calls it) continue some 37 years after Christ nailed the Law to the cross, and postpones the "ministration of life and righteousness" 37 years too long! People dead in sin had been made alive in Christ, the unrighteous had been made righteous, for 37 years before Jerusalem was destroyed. Among a host of Scriptures on the subject, consider Gal. 3:8, 21, 22, 24.

The two covenants did not overlap for some 37 years. A change was made (Heb. 7:12). He took away the first in order to establish the second (10:9). By means of that second one, which replaced the first one, the Hebrew brethren had already been sanctified (9:10), years before A.D. 70. Even a *careless* student of the Bible can see that the cross of Christ, and not A.D. 70, is the turning point in God's scheme of redemption. That is why Paul told the Corinthians that they were in Christ Jesus, who had been made unto them wisdom from God, and righteousness and sanctification, and redemption (1 Cor. 1:30). Paul had gone to Corinth to preach Christ and Him crucified, and not the Preterist-View of Prophecy, and so, when he wrote them later he could say what he did in that above-mentioned text!

Our last article in this section will be on Daniel's 70 weeks. King leans heavily upon it.

The Preterist View Heresy (VIII)
XVII. 16 (22 Feb. 1973)

In this eighth and final article in a series on Max King's *The Spirit of Prophecy*, we notice briefly his case for Daniel's prophecy on the 70 weeks (9:24-27). King has much to say about this prophecy throughout his book and lectures. The interpretations of this prophecy are legion, and it is not within the province of this short article to go into detail on it. Whether one interprets it in the usual manner, considering it as Messianic (that is, that the 70 weeks, and the six items of v. 24, are fulfilled in Christ's first coming and death on the cross--with the additional fact added by Daniel that Jerusalem would be destroyed), or whether one follows King's "gap" theory (whereby a 30 year gap is put between the 69th and the 70th prophetical week, and the six items are fulfilled within the 7 year period between A. D. 63 and A. D. 70), still King's Preterist-View doctrine is as foreign to the teachings of the Scriptures as any other man-made doctrine. This has been amply shown in the previous seven articles. It would take seven times seventy to expose every perversion of scripture to be found in his book!

How anyone could have knowledge of the mission and work of the Messiah, Christ Jesus, and after reading Dan. 9:24, conclude that these six items were not fulfilled in His first coming and death on the cross, is beyond me. But, King has Christ coming at the end of the 69th week, and then by means of his "gap" theory jumps some 30 years distance, and gets these six items fulfilled between A.D. 63 and A.D. 70. The weakness of his interpretations shows most obviously in spots. For example, on p. 55 he is in trouble trying to fit in the cessation of the sacrifice and oblation. On p. 64 he has to get "righteousness" in too many years after Pentecost, so he invents some expressions and says, this "has reference to the time of Christ's coming when things would be so changed that righteousness would be the *eternal* state of the new world." What the destruction of Jerusalem in A. D. 70 had to do with working such drastic changes that righteousness would be no longer a non-eternal state, but rather an eternal state, he does not tell us. He cannot! It is just a convenient fabrication.

After leaning so heavily upon his "gap" theory, he has the audacity to refer to our "gap" between one's death and his receiving the glorified or spiritual body in the resurrection day! A-211

In defense of the "gap" theory, King before the Preachers' Meeting presented Job 3:6, "As for that night . . . let it not come into the number of the months." "He has cut off (referring to Jesus -- bhr) A.D. 32, and we have a gap between the 69th and the 70th week. One of the reasons for that gap is, Christ said, 'But of the day and hour knoweth no one, not even the angels of heaven, neither the Son, but the Father only.' (Matt. 24:36). Had there been no gap, even the disciples could have figured out from the basis of Daniel's 70 weeks exactly when the Lord was going to return in the destruction of Israel." After trying to make Job's sufferings typical of the church's persecution by the Jews before Jerusalem was destroyed, he admits, after citing Job 3:6, "this is the closest I can come in the Bible to show the gap."

But in his book King refers, in defense of his "gap" theory, to (1) the division which Daniel's prophecy makes between the first 69 and the 70th weeks. Yes, but it also makes a division between the first 7 and the next 62! King, where's the gap there? (2) Acts 3:19-21 (Christ's being in heaven after his ascension and until his return in A. D. 70 to restore all things! This is a "gap."); 2 Pet. 3:9,15 (the period of the longsuffering of God; i.e., between A. D. 33 and A. D. 70 -- the "gap"); Luke 19:41-44 (time elapsed between Christ's being cut off and Jerusalem's destruction); Matt. 24:36 and Acts 1:7 (the secrecy of the time would indicate that the 70th week would not follow immediately the other 69).

Well, these Scriptures mentioned just above by King have no bearing at all upon the issue of whether or not a 70-week unit should have a "gap" in it. King merely accommodates to his "gap" theory what these passages say, and actually perverts the meaning of Acts 3:19-21 and 2 Pet. 3:9, 15. We have already exposed him on 2 Pet. 3, and suffice it to say, with the apostle Peter, that the passage in Acts 3 had to do with those days (v. 24)!

So there is no more a "gap" between the 69th and 70th weeks, than between the first 7 and the next 62! Daniel said that 70 weeks were decreed (v. 24), but King says 69, plus a gap of several more, plus the 70th, were decreed. As there was no gap in the 70 years of captivity in Babylonia, so none is to be expected in this 70, prophetical-year, unit.

Were not these six items of Dan. 9:24 so *messianic* in nature, through and through, we might look to other interpretations which would harmonize with the Scriptures. But the Preterist-View of prophecy tears the entire Divine Library of 66 books to shreds! Premillennialism does not begin to pervert as many Scriptures as King's doctrine does, and yet he told the preachers: "I think the premillennial issues today are going to force us in this direction (to the Preterist-View -- bhr) if we successfully meet them."

Daniel's prophecy tells us (v. 25) that the first seven prophetical years would see the rebuilding of Jerusalem, and that at the end of the next 62 would come the Messiah. Then, after the 62-week period, two things would happen (v. 26): the Messiah would be cut off, and the city and the sanctuary would be destroyed. This verse does not tell us how long after the expiration of the 62-week period these two events would happen, but the next verse (27th) does tell us that in the 70th prophetical week (or seven-year period) the Messiah would make a firm covenant with many and in the midst of it (3 and one-half years) he would make the sacrifice and oblation to cease. This is when, evidently, he would be cut off, as referred to in the previous verse, because his death on the cross put an end to the Law and its priesthood (Heb. 7:12. Was not the veil of the temple rent on that occasion?) The additional information is given in v. 27 concerning the fact of Jerusalem's destruction. It is mentioned as following (how long is not stated) the expiration of the 70th week. So, by Daniel's prophecy the Jews could know that their capital city would be fully destroyed subsequent to the Messiah's being cut off. Both events are mentioned in v. 26, but in v. 27 only the one is mentioned as occurring in the 70th week: the death of the Messiah, because he was to make the covenant then, and of course he would have to make it before he died, or in his death.

In conclusion, I direct my readers' attention (King, note that "readers" is plural and "attention" is singular, and compare it to what you have done to Rom. 8:23 and Phil. 3:21, "our body"!) again to the fact that the whole basis of this Preterist-View heresy is a perversion of Paul's allegory in Gal. 4. Paul, through the Holy Spirit, no more made allegorical the detail of Ishmael and Isaac living in Abraham's household for a short time, than he did the detail of Isaac's being weaned! King goes beyond what Paul makes allegorical and misuses the purpose of the allegory which he, Paul, did present.

He then sets out to boldly force literal passages into his own mold of spiritualizing, and dares call one "fleshly" if he does not agree with him. He switches terms and plays with English words, and employs his sophistry in the most subtle of ways. He adds a word or phrase, or otherwise makes some small change, to misrepresent his opponent. He quotes only part of an authority which would appear to agree with his position, and thus leaves wrong impressions. He has built up his own peculiar lingo to support his doctrine. He ignores contexts wholesale, and presses them into his service. *His book is difficult to read and monotonously repetitious. Paragraph after paragraph is but a conglomeration of jumbled and unrelated references which he has arbitrarily applied to fit his doctrine.* No one, without King's help, would ever have guessed that inspired writers were trying to get such a message across!

It is not at all likely that one so committed to a false doctrine, as Brother Max King is, can be salvaged from it, but if anything can be done to rescue him, I pledge all the help I can give to that end. *Nothing would make me happier.*[9]

---

[9] Bill Reeves, Fredricktown, Ohio 43019, The Preterist View Heresy, " Truth Magazine XVII, 9-16 (4 Jan-22 Feb 1973): 133-35, 155-57, 169-71, 185-87, 199-201, 217-19, 233-35, & 248-49

CHAPTER 6
The A.D. 70 System of Kingism

(The Church)

The task before me in this series of articles is to examine the fallacies of the "Max King Doctrine." Some may yet be unaware what the "Max King Doctrine" is. Briefly stated, it is the fanciful theory (heresy) that all the things for which we look to occur in the future have already come to pass. Those things that brethren have, since the first century, believed and taught (which the Bible so clearly sets forth) that will occur at the Lord's second coming, were all fulfilled in the destruction of Jerusalem in the year of 70 A.D. As wild a dream as your imagination will allow, can you believe the **Lord's second coming** is in the distant past, not the future? Can you believe the **resurrection of all the dead** has already occurred? Will you likewise believe that the **judgment** and the **end of the world** had its fulfillment in the first century? Also, will you permit yourself to believe the **church,** the kingdom prophesied throughout the Old Testament, was not really established on the day of Pentecost in Acts 2 in its fullness, glory, and power? This heresy says the church began in 70 A.D. when the city of Jerusalem was conquered and destroyed!

BACKGROUND

The subject of this study is known by a number of terms and phrases: The A.D. 70 Doctrine, Realized Eschatology, Kingism or the Max King Doctrine. Each of these are all designations of this wild, reckless, and foolhardy heresy. It is referred to as the "A.D. 70 Doctrine" because it seeks its fulfillment in the year A.D. 70. It is claimed that all the Bible foretold to occur in the future was fulfilled in A.D. 70 when the city of Jerusalem was destroyed. "Realized Eschatology" has to do with the fulfillment of "final" or "last" things.

> a. The word "eschatology" is a compound word of two Greek forms: *eschatos,* which is the word for last or final things; and, the word *logos,* which means something said or taught (instruction). *Logos* is commonly translated by our English term "word." Therefore,

"eschatology" has to do with the Bible's teaching of those things that have to do with the "end of time."

b. The word "realized" suggests the concept that something has already happened or occurred. If something is yet future, then it has not been realized. Things which are in the past have been realized.

c. Therefore, to speak of "realized eschatology" simply identifies that all those things which have to do with the end of time, the future, have already been realized or come to pass.

It is called **"Kingism"** or the **"Max King Doctrine"** because this teaching has been popularized by a man whose name is Max King who was once a faithful Gospel preacher. King debated the late Gus Nichols in July, 1973. The proposition King affirmed was: "The Holy Scriptures teach that the second coming of Christ, including the establishment of the eternal kingdom, the day of judgment, the end of the world, and the resurrection of the dead, occurred with the fall of Judaism in A.D. 70."

IMMEDIATE REACTION

Each one that first hears of this fanatical illusion cannot believe their ears! Their thought is that this is so far fetched, ridiculous, ludicrous, absurd, preposterous, asinine, outrageous, and wild, how would or could anyone be persuaded by it? Immediate questions arise, "if the end of the world has already occurred, then what are we doing here?" "If the resurrection of the dead is long past, why are the cemeteries still full?" Good questions! But as unbelievable as it is, we know by experience that however ridiculous or absurd a teaching might be, no matter how contradictory to clear and plain passages, some people will believe it and promote it. This doctrine is no exception. It has captured the attention and ensnared in its tentacles of error a number of our own brethren. It appears to be gaining ground in some areas. Therefore, it is necessary that we spend some time studying it so that we may be able to help those who may be enticed by it and others who have already been caught in its trap. Hopefully, we will be able to snatch some *"out of the fire"* while there is yet time (cf. Jude 1:23). I want to examine five major doctrines (as outlined above) in a series of five articles. The first one will be concerning the church.

THE CHURCH WAS NOT ESTABLISHED ON PENTECOST, 33 A.D.

The church was not established on Pentecost, 33 A.D., as is commonly believed so say the proponents of Kingism. What they actually say is that the kingdom did come on Pentecost, but not in its glory and power, it was not complete until A.D. 70. Nothing is further from the truth according to the Bible! In the *Spirit of Prophecy,* a book by Max R. King in which he sets forth his doctrine, we offer the following quotes. When discussing why it is error to tie together Mark 9:1 and Acts 1:8 he says: *"The kingdom was to come with power, and Acts 1:8 does not mention kingdom." "The apostles' question and the Lord's answer concerning the kingdom, places its coming in power beyond Pentecost"* (page 138). *"Mark 9:1 is parallel with Mathew. 16:27-28." "Instead of coming in his kingdom on Pentecost, Christ had gone to receive it"* (page 139). *"There is nothing contained in Dan. 2:44 that makes Pentecost the necessary date of its fulfillment"* (p.140). (Burleson, Ken, *8th Annual Seek The Old Paths Lectures,* East Corinth Church of Christ, Corinth, Miss., July 1993, pages 49-50). King plainly says that *"Christ did not come in his kingdom with power on Pentecost"* (page 138) yet on the next page he says, *"Pentecost was the beginning of his kingdom, but the fall of Jerusalem was the climatic state of its development and manifestation in power, glory, and judgment"* (page 139). The refutation of this teaching is simple, though not accepted by Kingites. It is obvious that whatever Scripture refutes their doctrine must be explained away and so they make such an attempt as is seen in the quotes above with Mark 9:1. Mark 9:1 coupled with Acts 1:8 and Acts 2:4 has been used effectively by the Lord's people since the establishment of the church/kingdom on the day of Pentecost. Jesus said, "...Verily I say unto you, That there be some of them that stand here, which shall not taste of death, till they have seen the kingdom of God come with power" (Mark 9:1). The pronouncement of the Lord was that the kingdom would *"come with power."* The kingdom (which is the church, Matthew 16:18-19) would make its appearance with power, i.e., be accompanied with power. Therefore, to learn when the kingdom came is to know when the power came; or to learn when the power came is to learn when the kingdom came. Both the kingdom and power would come at the same time. In Luke 24:49 Jesus said, "And, behold, I send the promise of my Father upon you: but tarry ye in the city of Jerusalem, until ye be endued *with power* from on high." On the day Jesus ascended up into heaven He told His apostles to wait in Jerusalem until they received the promise of the Father which they had heard of Him (Acts 1:4). "When they therefore were come together, they asked of Him, saying, Lord, wilt thou at this time restore again the kingdom to Israel?" Jesus said, "But ye shall *receive power,* after that the Holy Ghost is come upon you..." (Acts 1:6-8). With this passage, we learn the Holy Ghost (Holy Spirit) would come upon the apostles when they received power; and they would receive power when the Holy Spirit came. To receive the one (power) was to receive the other (Holy Spirit). "Rightly dividing" (cf. 2 Timothy 2:15) these verses is to learn that the *"kingdom"* was to come *"with power"* (Mark 9:1) and the power would come with the *"Holy Spirit"* (Acts 1:8). To learn when any one of the three came is to learn when all three came. Acts two reveals when the Holy Spirit came. The twelve apostles were assembled in Jerusalem on the first Pentecost after the resurrection of Jesus. [2]"And suddenly there came a sound from heaven as of a rushing mighty wind, and it filled all the house where they were sitting. [3]And there appeared unto them cloven tongues like as of fire, and it sat upon each of them. [4]And *they were all filled with the Holy Ghost,* and began to speak with other tongues, as the Spirit gave them utterance" (Acts 2:2- 4). The Holy Spirit had come upon them! They received power to speak in languages they had never learned (along with other miracles) and the kingdom was established—all at the same time. [41]"Then they that gladly received his word were baptized: and the same day there were added unto them about three thousand souls. [47]Praising God, and having favour with all the people. And *the Lord added to the church* daily such as should be saved" (Acts 2:41, 47). The kingdom/church came on Pentecost! Did the kingdom have its full glory and power on Pentecost? Kingites say "no." However, read the following verses and judge for yourself. Colossians 1:13 states that when one becomes a Christian, he/she is delivered from the "power of darkness" and translated into the "kingdom of his dear Son." Does this mean a sinner was removed from the power of Satan but was void of the power of the kingdom for the first 40 years of the kingdom's existence? That would be the case if the kingdom did not come in its full glory and power until A.D. 70! The next chapter plainly says these brethren were "complete" in Christ (Colossians 2:10). To be complete means to be full. How could Christians be complete or full, when according to Kingism, they were members of a kingdom which was not complete or full until A.D. 70? Further, Colossians 1:9-12 speaks of being "... *filled* with the knowledge of his will in *all wisdom and spiritual understanding;* [10]... *all pleasing,* being *fruitful in every good work...* [11]Strengthened with *all might,* according to his *glorious power,* unto *all patience* and *longsuffering* with *joyfulness;* [12]...made us meet to be partakers of the inheritance of the saints in light." These were all long before A.D. 70! Jesus said to the apostles, [29]"...I appoint unto you a kingdom... [30]That ye may eat and drink at my table in my kingdom..." (Luke 22:29-30). The table of the Lord was the Lord's Supper that every congregation took part in every first day of the week (Acts 20:7). The Corinthian church/kingdom were partakers of the table of the Lord (1 Corinthians 10:16-17). In verse 21 they were even rebuked when we read, "Ye cannot drink the cup of the Lord, and the cup of devils: ye cannot be partakers of the Lord's table, and of the table of devils." But when congregations partook of the Lord's Supper for 40 years prior to A.D. 70, was the kingdom, in which the table of the Lord existed, a glory less and powerless kingdom? If so, where is the evidence to support such? The fact is, none can be found! Ephesians 3:10 makes clear that the church was in its fullness before A.D. 70. "To the intent that *now* unto the principalities and powers in heavenly places might be known by the church *the manifold wisdom of God.*" God's manifold wisdom was THEN being made known by the church. The text says NOW, not in the future. This was before A.D. 70! The apostle Peter was given the keys to the kingdom (Matthew 16:18-19). The keys were used on Pentecost, A.D. 33 according to Acts 2. *But if Kingism be true, the keys were not used until A.D. 70. By this time, practically all the apostles were dead!*

The Final Judgment Occurred in A.D. 70

According to the *Spirit of Prophecy* (page 68), "This was the end of the world, the destruction of the temple, and the coming of Christ (Matthew 24:1-3). This was when heaven and earth passed away (Matthew 24:35; Revelation 20:11)."

The blunder of Kingism in this doctrine is that they take every passage which speaks of judgment and relegate it to a local, political, or temporal judgment.

The Bible often speaks of "judgment" in the sense of a localized or temporal judgment. God often speaks of bringing judgment upon different nations, cities, and people because of their wickedness. God brought judgment upon Sodom and Gomorrah (Genesis chapters 18-19), Egypt (Exodus 12:12), Moab (Jeremiah 48), Edom (Obadiah 1), Nineveh (Jonah 1-4) and many others.

On the other hand, the word "judgment" is often used in the sense of the final, universal judgment. The demands of many Scriptures cannot be met without a universal judge, Jesus Christ, and a universal gathering of all men and women that have lived since Adam and Eve. Scriptures from both the Old and New Testaments speak of such a final, future judgment.

In the Old Testament we read, "Therefore the ungodly shall not stand *in the judgment,* nor sinners in the congregation of the righteous." "And *he shall judge the world* in righteousness, *he shall minister judgment* to the people in uprightness" (Psalm 1:5; 9:8). "Rejoice, O young man, in thy youth; and let thy heart cheer thee in the days of thy youth, and walk in the ways of thine heart, and in the sight of thine eyes: but know thou, that for all these things *God will bring thee into judgment."* "For *God shall bring every work into judgment,* with every secret thing, whether it be good, or whether it be evil" (Ecclesiastes 11:9; 12:14).

In the New Testament we read, "...That every idle word that men shall speak, they shall give account thereof *in the day of judgment"* (Matthew 12:36). If the "day of judgment" here is referring to the destruction of Jerusalem, then where does that leave us? Does this verse have nothing to say to men today? It could only fit the future, final, universal judgment!

Jesus worked many mighty miracles in the cities of Chorazin and Bethsaida but they did not repent. "Woe unto thee, Chorazin! woe unto thee, Bethsaida! for if the mighty works, which were done in you, had been done in Tyre and Sidon, they would have repented long ago in sackcloth and ashes. But I say unto you, It shall be more tolerable for Tyre and Sidon *at the day of judgment,* than for you" (Matthew 11:21-22). If this "day of judgment" is the destruction of Jerusalem, what could it possibly have to do with the people of Tyre and Sidon who had been dead for centuries? The Lord plainly said it would be easier, i.e., more tolerable, for the people of Tyre and Sidon "at the day of judgment" than for those among whom He worked miracles. It's impossible that the day of judgment here could be the destruction of Jerusalem. Would the Lord resurrect the people of those ancient cities and place them in Jerusalem in A.D. 70 to experience the holocaust brought upon it by Titus the Roman General and the empire of Rome? Nonsense! There is a last, final, universal, and future judgment day.

When Paul spoke on Mar's Hill in Athens he said, "And the times of this ignorance God winked at; but now commandeth *all men every where* to repent: Because he hath *appointed a day,* in the which he will judge the world in righteousness by that man whom he hath ordained; whereof he hath given assurance unto all men, in that he hath raised him from the dead" (Acts 17:30-31). Were "all men every where" in the entire world in Jerusalem in A.D. 70? They couldn't be! Therefore, there is a future, universal, judgment day coming! This will be in "a day," not days or whole year.

There is a judgment seat upon which Jesus Christ sits. Someday, yet in the future from now, every person in the world will stand before the throne of Christ and be judged according to how he/she has lived. "For we must *all appear before the judgment seat of Christ;* that every one may receive the things done in his body, according to that he hath done, whether it be good or bad. Knowing therefore the terror of the Lord, we persuade men..." (2 Corinthians 5:10-11). If these verses were fulfilled in the destruction of Jerusalem, then they mean nothing to us—it is useless for us to preach them! Why would we persuade men to obey the gospel if there is no future judgment?

To the church at Rome Paul said, *"...we shall all stand before the judgment seat of Christ. For... every knee shall bow to me, and every tongue shall confess to God. So then every one of us shall give account of himself* to God" (Romans 14:10-12). We might as well cut these verses out of the Bible, for they mean nothing if they were fulfilled in 70 A.D.

Hebrews 9:27-28 makes the final judgment clear. "And as it is appointed unto men once to die, but *after this the judgment:* So Christ was once offered to bear the sins of many; and unto them that look for him shall he appear the second time without sin unto salvation." The judgment, according to Kingism, came upon Jerusalem in A.D. 70 while men were still living in the city. The judgment mentioned in Hebrews 9:27 would be after death, not before it. If that were not enough, we note that many people survived the destruction of the city—they did not die. Did judgment come upon them? According to Kingism it did! And it came while they were alive, not dead. Kingism contradicts these verses!

Second Peter 2:4 says "...God spared not the angels that sinned, but cast them down to hell, and delivered them into chains of darkness, *to be reserved unto judgment."* Were these angels reserved unto the judgment that came upon Jerusalem in A.D. 70? Were they in Jerusalem? Don't think so! Verse nine says God holds the wicked "unto the day of judgment to be punished." Were all the world's wicked brought into Jerusalem to be punished? You can't find it in the Scriptures!

In Revelation 20:10-15, the judgment scene is depicted where all the dead, small and great, stand before God and are judged. The devil is said to have been cast into the lake of fire and shall be tormented day and night for ever and ever. Before this, he worked his diabolical scheme among men, but now he is removed from the scene and cast into the lake of fire. If this happened in A.D. 70, then he would not be in the earth today to continue his work. But he is among men! Therefore, there is a future, universal, judgment of God when Satan will be cast into the lake of fire.

The Resurrection of All the Dead Occurred in A.D. 70

"The author sincerely believes that the general resurrection belongs to the same time and event as given to the coming of Christ, the judgment, end of the world, and receiving of the eternal kingdom." "This text deals with spiritual, not physical death, which is fairly evident from the context. The quickening power of God and Christ (John 5:19-23) has to do with spiritual regeneration." (Max King, *Spirit of Prophecy,* pages 212, 219)

The teaching of Kingism says that the references to the resurrection in the New Testament have to do with a spiritual resurrection and not a resurrection of the body. Their view is that the church of Christ which began on Pentecost (33 A.D.), was stifled, repressed, restrained by the Old Law of Moses. The Lord's church, they say, ran concurrently with the Law of Moses until the destruction of Jerusalem in A.D. 70. At that time, the body of the church was "resurrected" (in a spiritual sense) from the shackles of Judaism and received in its full glory and power. Therefore, references to the resurrection have to do with the spiritual resurrection of Christianity.

Again, with this teaching comes the immediate question, "If the resurrection of all the dead occurred at the destruction of Jerusalem, then where are they now and what are we that are alive doing here? Why are the graveyards still full and men around the world continue, day by day, to populate them even more?" Good questions!

The Holy, inspired Scriptures easily refutes this wild and reckless doctrine. Jesus said, "Marvel not at this: for the hour is coming, in the which *all that are in the graves* shall hear his voice, ²⁹And *shall come forth;* they that have done good, unto the resurrection of life; and they that have done evil, unto the resurrection of damnation" (John 5:28-29). As per Kingism, this is a reference to the church under the persecuting domination of Judaism. But this Scripture speaks of "all" that are in the graves. Literally, two Greek words are used in this verse, both of which are plural, saying *"all those"* in the tombs. Question, is the church plural? Were there *churches* being smothered by Judaism? No, the church is one body, not many (Ephesians 4:4; 1 Corinthians 12:13)If that were not enough, consider this: was the church "dead" for the first 40 years of its existence? Did the Lord establish dead, lifeless bodies (the church) which would be resurrected from the graves (tombs, plural) in A.D. 70? Imagine, the Lord died and shed His blood in order to purchase and establish a dead religious system that consisted of "bodies" (plural) and placed in "graves" (plural) to be resurrected 40 years later! Who can believe it?

Further, there are two classes of "all those" that will be resurrected from the "graves" in John 5:28-29: some have done good while others have done evil. Each class of "all those" (individuals, plural) will receive that which is due them. There's no way in the world to arrive at any other conclusion than to understand that this verse identifies a general resurrection of "all those" that have lived upon the earth, from Adam and Eve, to the last person in the world.

Between A.D. 30 and A.D. 70, was there a good church(es) and an evil church(es)? Were both resurrected and each received that which was due them? Outrageous! This text cannot be explained in any way other than a general resurrection of "all those" dead ones (bodies) who have been buried in "graves" around the world since the beginning of time.

In writing to the church at Corinth, Paul discusses at length the resurrection of the dead (1 Corinthians 15). He establishes the fact of the Lord's death, burial, and resurrection from the grave (verses 1-11). The brethren there believed and accepted that fact. However, in verse 12 we read, "Now if Christ be preached that he rose from the dead, how say some among you that there is no resurrection of the dead?" The Holy Spirit emphatically sets forth, in the remainder of the chapter, the fact that those who have died will one day be raised from the dead just as Christ was raised from the dead. Christ's bodily resurrection is used as a comparison or likeness of our own bodily resurrection. Heaven's argument is, [13]...if there be no resurrection of the dead, then is Christ not risen: [14]And if Christ be not risen, then is our preaching vain, and your faith is also vain. [15]Yea, and we are found false witnesses of God; because we have testified of God that he raised up Christ: whom he raised not up, if so be that the dead rise not. [16]For if the dead rise not, then is not Christ raised: [17]And if Christ be not raised, your faith is vain; ye are yet in your sins. [18]Then they also which are fallen asleep in Christ are perished. [19]If in this life only we have hope in Christ, we are of all men most miserable. [20]But now is Christ risen from the dead, and become the firstfruits of them that slept. [21]For since by man came death, by man came also the resurrection of the dead. [22]For as in Adam all die, even so in Christ shall all be made alive. [23]But every man in his own order: Christ the firstfruits; afterward they that are Christ's at his coming" (1 Corinthians 15:13-23).

One day, yet in the future, those who have died will come out of their graves and stand before the Lord to be judged (2 Corinthians 5:10)! Our body will be changed! It will not be the body that was buried for flesh and blood cannot inherit the kingdom of heaven (1 Corinthians 15:36-58). None the less, there will be a bodily resurrection of all the dead. Every verse in this text makes plain that what is under consideration are humans, people, those who once lived and have died. There's no way the church is spoken of here because it is alive and singular, not dead and plural. The church does not have now, nor has ever had, "flesh and blood" (cf. verse 50). Adam (a living human being) died even as all humans die as a consequence of his sin. Through Christ, all (along with Adam) will one day be made alive (verse 22).

Christ is referred to as the "firstfruits" of them that sleep (verses 20-23). That is, Christ was the first to be raised from the dead never to die again. For Him to be the first, implies there were others to follow. That is the argument and point of First Corinthians 15. But if the resurrection occurred in A.D. 70 and it was only a "spiritual" resurrection, then that necessitates the Lord's resurrection was only a spiritual resurrection—that He did not literally, bodily, rise from the grave! But He did rise from the grave! He walked, talked, and ate with the apostles (John 21). He showed them the scars in his hands, feet, and side (cf. Luke 24:39-40; John 20:20- 27).

The Lord's resurrection from the grave is proof of our future resurrection from the grave (1 Corinthians 15:12-22). "But every man in his own order: Christ the firstfruits; *afterward they that are Christ's at his coming"* (1 Corinthians 15:23). It is inconceivable to imagine how some say the resurrection is past already—long ago in 70 A.D. and, that it was the spiritual resurrection of the church from under the suppression of Judaism.

The Bible often speaks of departures from the truth and provides ample information to refute such damnable doctrines. Error concerning the final, universal, resurrection from the dead is nothing new in our generation. There were even those as far back as the first century that believed and taught damnable error with regard to the resurrection. Two men especially were immortalized in heaven's book, the Bible, in calling their names and marking them for their error for all time. Read it, [16]"But shun profane and vain babblings: for they will increase unto more ungodliness. [17]And their word will eat as doth a canker: *of whom is Hymenaeus and Philetus;* [18]*Who concerning the truth have erred, saying that the resurrection is past already; and overthrow the faith of some"* (2 Timothy 2:16-18; Romans 16:17-18). Notice: saying the resurrection has already occurred is a doctrine of no little consequence. Those who so believe and teach have left the faith and overthrow the faith of others! It is not and can not be an optional matter to deny the final resurrection of all the dead. It is a matter of faith—a matter of fellowship —a matter of heaven or hell. To deny the future resurrection of all the dead is to deny the resurrection of Christ and to deny the resurrection of Christ makes salvation impossible and our preaching to be vain (1 Corinthians 15:12-19).

The End of the World Occurred in A.D. 70

Before you question my sanity at the above heading, please take note that the system of "Realized Eschatology" teaches the world ended in A.D. 70. Of course you are probably now shaking your head and thinking, if that is so, what are we doing here? What has been going on the past 1,900 years? If there is no future end of the world, will the earth continue on and on? What's going on here?

Kingism says,

> This was the end of the world, the destruction of the temple, and the coming of Christ (Matthew 24:1-3). This was when heaven and earth passed away (Matthew 24:35; Revelation 20:11). *(Spirit of Prophecy,* p.68).

A.D. 70 advocates make the references to the "end of the world" equivalent to the end of the "Jewish age." But as we have seen in previous points, their forced interpretations will not hold up.

Matthew 24 is so clear and discerning as to the descriptions of both the destruction of Jerusalem in A.D. 70 (verses 4-34) and the end of the world (yet future; verses 24:35; 25:30) that it is hard to conceive how anyone can miss it. In verse one we read, "And Jesus went out, and departed from the temple: and his disciples came to him for to show him the buildings of the temple. ²And Jesus said unto them, See ye not all these things? verily I say unto you, There shall not be left here one stone upon another, that shall not be thrown down. ³And as he sat upon the mount of Olives, the disciples came unto him privately, saying, Tell us, *when shall these things be?* and *what shall be the sign of thy coming,* and of *the end of the world"* (Matthew 24:1-3)?

In Matthew 24:4, Jesus begins to answer their questions. He begins telling when these things shall be and what "signs" to notice that will signal the approaching destruction. When the Christians observed these signs they were to escape to the mountains—leave Jerusalem. But in regards to the end of the world, there would be no "signs" given, for escape will not be possible! In verse 34 Jesus says, "...This generation shall not pass, till all these things be fulfilled." Everything preceding verse 34 would come to pass in "that generation" and there would be sign after sign to indicate its arrival. However, a sure and marked contrast to the destruction of Jerusalem is discussed beginning in verse 35. Whereas regarding the destruction of Jerusalem there were "signs" to watch for so that one would know when to leave the city; but concerning the end of the world, no signs would be given. "But of that day and hour knoweth no man, no, not the angels of heaven, but my Father only" (verse 36). If "that day and hour" (verse 36) is discussing the same event as "this generation" (verse 34), then there is a certain and irreconcilable contradiction. The remainder of the chapter, as well as chapter 25, gives one example after another to show there would be NO "signs" or "warnings" as to when the end of the world would occur.

When the end of the world comes, it will be without warning. There will be absolutely no indication that such is about to happen. Notice the examples Jesus used to illustrate this truth: 1) Business will be as usual among men, just as it was when the flood came (24:37-41); 2) No one knows when a thief may break into his house (24:42-44); 3) A master comes home unannounced to recompense to his servants their due (24:45-51); 4) The 10 virgins had no indication when the bridegroom would come to take them to the wedding (25:1-13); 5) The man who travelled into a far country and left his goods with his servants gave no indication when He would return.

This physical world in which we now live and the entire material universe will one day be destroyed so that it will no longer exist. By inspiration, the apostle Peter, very ably and plainly said, in talking about this physical world, [7]"But the heavens and the earth, which are now, by the same word are kept in store, reserved unto fire against the day of judgment and perdition of ungodly men. [10]But the day of the Lord will come as a thief in the night; in the which the heavens shall pass away with a great noise, and the elements shall melt with fervent heat, the earth also and the works that are therein shall be burned up. [11]Seeing then that all these things shall be dissolved, what manner of persons ought ye to be in all holy conversation and godliness, [12]Looking for and hasting unto the coming of the day of

God, wherein the heavens being on fire shall be dissolved, and the elements shall melt with fervent heat" (2 Peter 3:7, 10-12). He is plainly talking about this physical world (2 Peter 3:3-6). As the flood of water in Noah's day destroyed the earth, the day is yet future when "fervent heat" will melt the earth, all the works that are in it, and all elements of the universe. Everything will be dissolved (verses 10-11)! There's no way to strain a spiritual fulfillment out of this text!

Hebrews one discusses the majesty and deity of Jesus the Christ. It reveals that God, through Jesus, made the worlds (material universe) "in the beginning" and maintains them by the power of His Word (1:2-3, 10; cf. Genesis 1:1). Jesus is eternal (1:8), but His creation, the "worlds," are temporary. [11] "They shall perish; but thou remainest; and they all shall wax old as doth a garment; [12] And as a vesture shalt thou fold them up, and they shall be changed: but thou art the same, and thy years shall not fail" (1:11-12).

A.D. 70 theorists take Hebrews one and say that it refers to the end of the Mosaic age, not the material universe, just as they do all passages which speak of the "end-time!" But such is the plight of those who have an agenda to maintain. In the case of Kingites, they must take every passage that speaks of future things and twist them around to fit their doctrine that every Bible prophecy of "end things" was fulfilled in A.D. 70. On this point in Hebrews one, brother Wayne Jackson comments.

> In verse 10, when the record says, "And thou, Lord, in the beginning didst lay the foundation of the earth, and the heavens are the works of thy hands," is there anybody in his right mind who is going to read this passage in this fashion: "And thou, Lord, in the beginning of the Mosaic dispensation, didst lay the foundation of the earth, that is, you established the law of Moses; and the heaven, that is, the ordinances of the law, are the works of your hands?" To interpret that as the Jewish law has to be the biggest bunch of theological garbage that I have ever been exposed to in my life. It is pure foolishness. *(The A.D. 70 Theory, A Review of the Max King Doctrine,* Jackson, Wayne, Courier Publications, Stockton, CA, 1990, pages 77-78)

Revelation 20:11-15 reveals the judgment scene in which heaven and earth *"fled away; and there was found no place for them."* All the dead, small and great, wherever they were, stood before the throne and were judged according to their works. Where did such occur when Jerusalem was destroyed? Were the dead, which had died at sea, resurrected and brought to Jerusalem to be judged? Were the dead in the Hadean realm resurrected in 70 A.D. to stand before the Lord's throne in Jerusalem? Strain as hard as you might and you will not find it here!

The Second Coming of Christ Occurred in A.D. 70

According to the Max King doctrine, we read:

> There is no time period between the fall of Jerusalem and the second coming of Christ. They are synchronous events time-wise. ... There is no scriptural basis for extending the second coming of Christ beyond the fall of Judaism. *(The Spirit of Prophecy,* pages 81, 105).

In his debate with Gus Nichols, King said:

> I affirm the VISIBLE coming of Jesus Christ in the destruction of Jerusalem. And I affirm the ACTUAL coming, and the REAL coming of Jesus Christ in the destruction of Jerusalem (page 48). ... *I affirm that Jesus came REALLY and TRULY and ACTUALLY and VISIBLY the second* time (page 49)!

As with the other points of departure from the Truth in the Kingism Cult, the idea of the Lord's second and final coming occurring in A.D. 70 is shocking and shameful. And, like the other points we have examined, is easily shown to be utterly false from the Scriptures.

That the second coming of Christ has NOT occurred, and is yet in the future, is clearly set forth in many passages. We shall examine a few.

Hebrews 9:28 is the only text that specifically uses the word "second" in referring to the Lord's coming again after He left the earth in Acts 1:9-11. "So Christ was once offered to bear the sins of many; and unto them that look for him shall he appear the **second time** without sin unto salvation." The Lord's appearance the "first time" was a literal appearance. He shall appear the "second time" in a literal appearance. His second appearance will not be a spiritual or figurative appearance.

The Lord will come the "second time" to: raise the dead (John 5:28-29; Acts 24:15), judge the world (Matthew 25:31-46; Romans 14:10-12; Acts

17:31), sentence the wicked (2 Thessalonians 1:7-9), reward the righteous (Revelation 22:2; Matthew 25:46), and deliver up the kingdom (church) to the Father (1 Corinthians 15:24). According to Kingism, all these have already taken place in A.D. 70!

Let's note what the Bible says will occur when the Lord comes again. If these things have not come to pass, then we know the Lord has not come again. That ought to be simple enough.

First Corinthians 15:23-24 says that when the Lord comes again, "**... Then cometh the end,** when he shall have delivered up the kingdom to God, even the Father; when he shall have put down all rule and all authority and power." The kingdom is His church. And since the church/kingdom is still in existence today, the Lord either has not come or failed to do that which this verse says He would do. The Lord's purpose cannot fail. Therefore, the Lord has not come!

This passage also says that when He comes He would "have put down all rule and all authority and all power." However, authorities and powers still exist today and remain under the influence of Satan (cf. Ephesians 6:12). Therefore, the Lord has not come.

Further, the text here says the Lord will raise the dead—all will be "made alive" (verse 22) at His coming (verse 23). Yet the cemeteries are still full and mourners continue to bury their dead day by day. Therefore, the Lord has not come.

In Philippians 3:20-21 we read, "For our conversation is in heaven; from whence also we look for the Saviour, the Lord Jesus Christ: Who shall change our vile body, that it may be fashioned like unto his glorious body, according to the working whereby he is able even to subdue all things unto himself." The Lord is now in heaven and has a glorious body—not the body He had on earth. When He comes again, He will change our vile body, the body we have now, to be like His—a glorious body (cf. 1 Corinthians 15:35-54). But we still have our vile body—the body of our humiliation, our low estate. Therefore, the Lord has not come.

Second Thessalonians 2:1-12. Some at the church in Thessalonica apparently had the mistaken idea that the Lord's second coming was "at hand"—that it was near or soon. Paul wrote them concerning the "coming of our Lord Jesus Christ" (verse 1), the "day of Christ" (verse 2) saying,

"Let no man deceive you by any means: for *that day shall not come, except there come a falling away first...*" (verse 3). Here is a prediction of a "falling away" —a general and major departure from the Truth. The text clearly says the Lord will not come until this departure from the Truth comes first. It is believed this was written in late 53 or early 54 A.D. If the Lord came in 70 A.D., then there had to have been a "falling away"—an apostasy—of the Lord's church between 54 A.D. and 70 A.D. There is no record of a "falling away" during that time. Therefore, the Lord did not come in A.D. 70. The "falling away" came, as we all know, in the forming and existence of the Catholic Church which recognized its first pope in 606 A.D.

In **Second Thessalonians chapter one,** Paul mentions the hardships and persecutions inflicted upon the brethren (verses 4-5). He reveals there will be a time when they will be able to rest from such tribulation when He says, "And to you who are troubled rest with us, **when the Lord Jesus shall be revealed from heaven** with his mighty angels..." (verse 7). When would they be able to rest? When "the Lord Jesus shall be revealed from heaven" He will inflict punishment upon those who "know not God" and those who "obey not the gospel" (verse 8). Are the saints of God today at rest? Do they still suffer persecution? Yea verily! Therefore, the Lord has not yet come.

In **First Corinthians 11:26,** Paul said, in speaking of the Lord's Supper, "For as often as ye eat this bread, and drink this cup, *ye do shew the Lord's death till he come.*" One of the purposes of eating the Lord's Supper is to "shew the Lord's death." How long will the saints of the church eat the Supper? They will eat it "till he come." Do we eat the Lord's Supper today? Yes. Therefore, the Lord has not come. If He came in A.D. 70, then saints of God have no business eating the Lord's Supper today. Do those who espouse the King doctrine eat the Lord's Supper? Yes.

John 14:1-3 holds great significance to the subject of the second coming. Jesus said, "...In my Father's house are many mansions: if it were not so, I would have told you. I go to prepare a place for you. And if I go and prepare a place for you, I will come again, and receive you unto myself; that where I am, there ye may be also." Jesus said when He comes again He would receive the disciples to be with Him in that place He was preparing for them. That place was in heaven, not on earth, for He said "I go" and "I will come again." Are we now in heaven or on earth? We are on earth. Therefore, the Lord has not come.

Matthew 25:31-46 describes the judgment scene that will take place "when the Son of man shall come." "All nations" will be gathered before the Lord to be judged. Were all nations gathered in Jerusalem in A.D. 70? Were those living in North and South America there? They are a part of all nations (cf. Revelation 5:9; 14:6). No, they were not there. The scene described in Matthew 25 has not yet occurred. Therefore, the Lord has not come.

Revelation 1:7 says, "Behold, he cometh with clouds; and every eye shall see him, and they also which pierced him: and all kindreds of the earth shall wail because of him. Even so, Amen." When the Lord "cometh with clouds," every eye, every person, would see him. Have you seen the Lord coming in the clouds? Neither have I. Therefore, the Lord has not come.

Matthew 16:27 says, "For the Son of man shall come in the glory of his Father with his angels; and then he shall reward every man according to his works." Have all men/women been rewarded for their works? The very fact that people continue to live on this globe is evidence that such has not occurred. You nor I have been rewarded according to our works. Therefore, the Lord has not come.

Need we continue? How many verses will it take to convince you that the Lord's second coming is yet future, not in the past?

The Real Significance of A.D. 70

Even though there is a great deal of error being circulated, believed, and taught relative to the destruction of Jerusalem which occurred in A.D. 70, that does not mean that sincere Bible students should seek to avoid what the Bible *does say* relative to that event. The destruction of Jerusalem in 70 A.D. is an historical event that cannot be denied. What significance did it have for those who lived in that day; and, what significance does it have for us today, if any? The fact that it is prophesied of in both the Old and New Testaments reveals that it does hold importance in God's scheme of things (cf. Zechariah 14; Matthew 24:4-34; Mark 13:5-30; Luke 21:8-31; 1 Peter 4:17-18).

In Genesis 12:1-7, God made a promise to Abraham that was three-fold: 1) "I will make of thee a great nation" (verse 2), 2) "in thee shall all families of the earth be blessed" (verse 3), 3) "Unto thy seed will I give this land" (verse 7). Through Abraham's grandson Jacob, whose name was changed to Israel, the "great nation" of Israel was born. God was carrying out His promise to Abraham in them. After leaving the bondage of Egypt, they were caused to possess the "land of Canaan" and live under the Law of Moses received at Mt. Sinai. Even then, there would come a day when the law given by Moses would end and a new prophet and law would be established (cf. Deuteronomy 18:15; Jeremiah 31:31-34; Acts 3:19-24). The Gentiles would be brought in as God's people along with the Israelites (cf. Isaiah 62:1-2; 65:1; Deuteronomy 32:21). A new law would be established that would encompass all tongues, peoples, and nations and cover the whole world. God sought to protect and provide for the nation of Israel through whom the promised Messiah would come. When the nation of Israel had accomplished its purpose, it would cease to have significance. The Law of Moses is plainly described as a "...schoolmaster to bring us unto Christ, that we might be justified by faith. But after that faith is come, we are no longer under a schoolmaster. For ye are all the children of God by faith in Christ Jesus" (Galatians 3:24-26).

Through the centuries of the nation of Israel, there were those who grew to love and count as their whole existence the fleshly nation of Israel. They clung so closely to it they could not conceive of it ending. They could not dream that it was only temporary. Even after God made known His will through the revelation of the Gospel (cf. Romans 16:25-26; Ephesians 3:1-11), the majority of Jews refused to let go of fleshly Israel with its law, sacrifices, and temple worship. God, in His infinite knowledge and wisdom, knew that such would be the case. There would, of necessity, have to be a cataclysmic event that would ultimately and finally cause the Jewish political, civil, and religious system to crumble and fall. The destruction of the city of Jerusalem, along with the temple and its sacrifices, was that devastating event. Through this means, God put a stop to all that the devout fleshly Jews held dear. No longer would any Jew be able to trace their lineage to Abraham. No one would be able to confirm from what tribe they descended. No priest could establish his right to offer sacrifices. All genealogical records had been destroyed!

The nation of Israel under the Law of Moses was unique in that the Israelites comprised the religious, political, and civil governments. Unlike today, the religious, political, and civil are each distinct and separate. The Lord's church is not a part of the political or civil system—and vice versa. But under the Law of Moses, such was not the case. Every Israelite was a child of God. Therefore, those who made up the political and civil systems were children of God just as those who officiated at religious services.

Each of these systems (political, civil, and religious) under the Law of Moses would end.

The death of Jesus on the cross in 33 A.D. marked the end of the religious system of the Law of Moses which was boldly proclaimed on Pentecost in Acts 2; and, the destruction of the city of Jerusalem in 70 A.D. ended the political and civil system of the Jews. Beyond A.D. 70, all hope of a future Messiah and an earthly political regime among the Jews was finally and forever crushed!

The destruction of Jerusalem was certainly a significant event. It impacted every facet of the Jewish political, civil, economic, and religious systems. It showed once and for all, to those who yet refused to believe, that God had ended His dealings with the Jews. In God's providence, He brought together events to demonstrate to the Jews that His Son's death on the cross had put an end to Judaism.

Another occasion where God intervened to accomplish His Will is at the conversion of the household of Cornelius (Acts 10-11). This event was designed to convince the Jews that the gospel was for the Gentiles also. This actually began on the day of Pentecost but was not fully carried out by the Lord's people until the baptizing of Cornelius. Likewise, the Law of Moses, along with all that attended it, ceased at the cross (Colossians 2:14) and the proclamation of it was preached on Pentecost, but it took the decisive event in A.D. 70 to convince many people that such was indeed the case.

CONCLUSION

The summary of the whole A.D. 70 system is aptly described by Wayne Jackson. "So brethren, the whole A.D. 70/King scenario is false. Christ did not affect His second coming in A.D. 70; the dead were not raised in A.D. 70; the judgment day did not occur with the destruction of Jerusalem; and the world did not end in A.D. 70. The entire theory of "realized eschatology" is false from start to finish."

"We deeply grieve that good brethren have been caught up in this foolish movement. It has produced much harm and no good. It is unsettling and divisive. The situation is, however, a commentary upon the extremes to which some will go in an attempt to make a name in history. It is further an example of how ill-informed many members of the church actually are;

they are ripe for the picking. The words of the ancient prophet are applicable even today—"My people are destroyed for a lack of knowledge." *(The A.D. 70 Theory, A Review of the Max King Doctrine,* Jackson, Wayne, Courier Publications, Stockton, CA, 1990, page 82)

This doctrinal theory of A.D. 70 is so fantastic, incredible, inconceivable, that it fits well with other religious systems that are likewise so far fetched and preposterous, they are unbelievable and easily refuted with the Scriptures. Systems such as: Mormonism, with their "God was once a man" doctrine and Jehovah Witnesses, with their idea that Jesus is not deity and man doesn't have a soul. I'm not trying to make light of those who believe the A.D. 70 doctrine, but I am seeking to show the utter nonsense of the doctrine itself.

May this brief study cause those who embrace Kingism to deeply examine and profoundly probe the doctrine they espouse and uphold. May it be the case they will see the error of their way and repent of this most serious error. We pray for the hastening of that day.[10]

---

[10] Garland Robinson Editor of Seek the Old Paths, 1996 and 1997, The A.D. 70 System of Kingism

CHAPTER 7
The Second Coming of Christ: Did it Already Occur?

Because of the serious effect this heresy has had upon individuals and entire churches, it is necessary that it be exposed for what it is—a perversion of the gospel of Christ (Galatians 1:6-9). To engage in such an endeavor is mandated in Scripture (Jude 3-4). It is always right to expose error, protect the innocent, and turn away from divisive doctrines (Romans 16:17-18). Our motive must be love for truth and for the souls of men. Our objective must be to warn and correct, using God's word as our standard (2 Timothy 2:24-26; 4:1-5).

During the Enumclaw lectureship mentioned above, Harry Osborne and Joe Price had an opportunity to discuss this subject with two men who defended the A.D. 70 doctrine. On that occasion, these men set forth the basic position of the doctrine, namely, that the final coming of Christ and the promised resurrection (1 Thessalonians 4:16; 1 Corinthians 15) occurred in 70 A.D. Such a doctrine has far-reaching consequences upon the faith of Christians! If it is true, then all who hope in the actual, bodily, personal return of Jesus are deceived (1 Thessalonians 4:16). If it is true, then we cannot expect our bodies to be raised to immortality when Jesus comes (1 Corinthians 15:22-23, 51-54). If this doctrine is false, then those holding it have erred, and are guilty of overthrowing the faith of others, *as were Hymenaeus and Philetus, who also* said "the resurrection is past already" (2 Timothy 2:16-18). There is no middle ground!

What is Realized Eschatology?

As James Orr says, "By 'eschatology,' or doctrine of last things, is meant the ideas entertained at any period on the future life, the end of the world (resurrection, judgment;...) and the eternal destinies of mankind" (International Standard Bible Encyclopedia, James Orr, II:972). "Realized" signifies accomplishment, hence, Realized Eschatology is a doctrine of completed last things. According to its interpretation of the Bible, the end times were realized and accomplished in 70 A.D. at the destruction of Jerusalem. In fact, we are told by a major proponent of this doctrine that "the fall of Judaism (and its far reaching consequences) is, therefore, a major subject of the Bible" (The Spirit of Prophecy, Max R. King, page 239). [For an excellent review and rebuttal of this book, see "The Preterist View Heresy (1-VIII)," Bill Reeves, Truth Magazine, Vol. XVII, No. 9-16 (4 January - 22 February, 1973).]

We are told that the second coming of Christ occurred at 70 A.D., at which time every spiritual blessing was perfected and made available to the world. Due to fundamental failures in sound, Biblical interpretation, Christians are being taught that all prophecy of end-time events was fulfilled in 70 A.D., and to look beyond that date for the personal coming of Christ and the bodily resurrection of mankind followed by a judgment is without Biblical authority. Here is a sampling of this basic viewpoint of the doctrine from King's *The Spirit of Prophecy*:

> There is no scriptural basis for extending the second coming of Christ beyond the fall of Judaism. - page 105

> ...the end of the Jewish world was the second coming of Christ. - page 81 (emp., King's)

> Prophecy found its complete fulfillment in the second coming of Christ, and now may be regarded as closed and consummated. - page 65

Thus, the second coming of Christ is made equal with the "fall of Judaism" (the destruction of Jerusalem in 70 A.D.). To King, and some misguided brethren today, we dare not look to our future in anticipation of the coming of the Lord! All prophecies relating to it were fulfilled in 70 A.D.! Now, when it is shown that the personal, bodily return of our Lord is described in terms which cannot apply to the events of 70 A.D., the error of this doctrine will be fully exposed.

Did Jesus Come In The First Century Following His Ascension?

There is ample evidence in the word of God that Jesus did indeed come *in some sense* (or senses) in the first century. For example, He came in His kingdom (Matthew 16:28) with power (Mark 9:1) on the day of Pentecost (Acts 1:4-5, 8; 2:1-4, 33). Now, look how Jesus described the sending of the promised Comforter (the Holy Spirit) in John 14:18: "I will come to you." Surely no one will conclude that this must mean a bodily coming of Jesus! How would He come? Not bodily, but representatively, through the

Holy Spirit whom He would send (John 15:26). Again, in Matthew 24:29-30, Jesus taught that during that generation (24:34) "they shall see the Son of man coming on the clouds of heaven with power and great glory." The context of Matthew 24 tells us how they would see Him. The context of the chapter is the destruction of Jerusalem. Unquestionably, Jesus did not appear bodily in 70 A.D. when Jerusalem fell. Instead, Matthew 24:30 speaks of His presence in Jerusalem's judgment. He authorized it, and brought it to pass (cf. Isaiah 19:1). They would see or discern His presence when this destructive judgment occurred.

Yes, Jesus Christ came in judgment in 70 A.D., but it was not His bodily return! Similar language is used to describe His coming in judgment against the powers persecuting the saints in Revelation 1:7 (cf. Revelation 19:11-21). None of these "comings" of the Lord prevent a future coming of Christ in bodily form at the end of time!

The A.D. 70 doctrine would make every mention of the "coming of the Lord" or "day of the Lord" mean the same event, regardless of its usage in context. It is a fact of Biblical interpretation that the same phrase can have different meanings. For example, take the expression "laid hands upon." In Acts 4:3, it means to arrest. In Acts 13:3, it means to commend. In Luke 13:13, it means to heal. In Acts 8:17 and 19:6, it means to impart spiritual gifts. To arbitrarily assign one meaning to this phrase every time it is used would result in absurdity! Yet this is exactly what the A.D. 70 doctrine does with "coming of the Lord" and "day of the Lord."

The problem with limiting the coming of the Lord to 70 A.D. is demonstrated by at least three passages in the New Testament:

1) Consider Acts 1:9-11, where angels tell the apostles that Jesus "shall so come in like manner as ye beheld him going into heaven" (verse 11, ASV). In what manner did Jesus go into heaven? Jesus ascended into heaven actually and personally, in His resurrected body (Luke 24:39). In Acts 1:9-11, five words are used which emphasize that actual sight was involved on this occasion. His apostles "were looking" as Jesus was taken up (verse 9). A cloud received Jesus "out of their sight" (verse 9). The apostles were "looking stedfastly into heaven" when two men in white apparel appeared to them (verse 10). These messengers asked the apostles, "Why stand ye looking into heaven?" (verse 11). And finally, the apostles were assured that Jesus would return in like manner as they had "beheld him" going into heaven (verse 11). The apostles actually saw Jesus' bodily ascension. This is the manner in which He will return (1 Thessalonians 4:16-

17). Jesus did not come in bodily form, nor was He personally seen in the events of the coming of the kingdom (Matthew 16:28; John 14:18), the destruction of Jerusalem in 70 A.D. (Matthew 24:30), or in the defeat of the persecuting powers of Revelation 1:7. Christ's personal, bodily return is yet future!

2) Next, consider 2 Peter 3:5-7, 10-11, where the A.D. 70 advocate "spiritualizes" away the meaning of the word of God. By His word, God created and then destroyed the world with water. By that same word of God, the heavens and earth which now exist are stored up for fire, awaiting a day of judgment against ungodliness:

> For this they willfully forget, that there were heavens from of old, and an earth compacted out of water and amidst water, by the word of God; by which means the world that then was, being overflowed with water, perished: but the heavens that now are, and the earth, by the same word have been stored up for fire, being reserved against the day of judgment and destruction of ungodly men. But the day of the Lord will come as a thief; in the which the heavens shall pass away with a great noise, and the elements shall be dissolved with fervent heat, and the earth and the works that are therein shall be burned up (2 Peter 3:5-7, 11).

The A.D. 70 advocates try to make the heavens and earth (verses 7, 10), which shall meet a fiery end, the Jewish economy (as do the Jehovah's Witnesses). But this is to no avail. The world which was overflowed with water is now stored up for fire. This fiery judgment shall occur on "the day of the Lord" (verse 10), at His "coming" (verse 4). Was the world of Noah's time actually flooded? Then the world which now exists shall actually be destroyed with fire! If this verse had been fulfilled in 70 A.D., none of us would be here!

The abuse of this passage illustrates the error in Biblical interpretation which is present in this system of error. As D. R. Dungan notes:

> Many seem disposed to regard themselves as at liberty to make anything out of the Bible which their theology may demand or their whims require. And if, at any time, they find a passage that will not harmonize with that view, then the next thing is to find one or more words in the text used elsewhere in a figurative sense, and then demand that such be the Biblical dictionary on the meaning of that word, and hence that it must be the meaning in that place. (Hermeneutics, Dungan, page 217)

The A.D. 70 doctrine attempts this with "the day of the Lord" and His "coming" in 2 Peter 3:4-11, but it finds no support here!

3) 1 Corinthians 15 teaches a future, bodily resurrection from the dead. While the A.D. 70 doctrine says the resurrection is past already (having occurred in 70 A.D.), this passage decisively refutes that claim. To the Realized Eschatologist, the *primary meaning* of 1 Corinthians 15 is the resurrection of Christianity out of Judaism, not the resurrection of mankind at the personal return of Jesus Christ. To briefly set forth their case, hear Max King on what is resurrected in 1 Corinthians 15:

"Next (1 Corinthians 15:35-44 - jrp), Paul answers questions concerning how the dead are raised and with what body they come forth. The *primary application* (emphasis, jrp) deals with the development and rise of the Christian system itself, with a secondary application belonging to believers and their state within the system. The natural body that was sown (verse 44) answers to the fleshly or carnal system of Judaism in which existed prophecies, types, and patterns from which came the spiritual body designed of God....The *natural body* (emp., King's), receiving its death blow at the cross and beginning then to wax old and decay (Hebrews 8:13), became a nursery or seed-body for the germination, growth, and development of the spiritual body by means of the gospel.

"Thus, *out of the decay of Judaism arose the spiritual body of Christianity* (emphasis, jrp) that became fully developed or resurrected by the end-time. Hence, this is the primary meaning of Paul's statement (emphasis, jrp), 'It is sown a natural body; it is raised a spiritual body. There is a natural body and there is a spiritual body'" (*The Spirit of Prophecy*, King, pages 199-200).

The assumed definitions and applications in that quotation alone show the subjective nature of this doctrine! The Scriptures are twisted to say what has already been decided, namely, that Christianity arose out of Judaism, an event which we are told was completed in 70 A.D.! I cannot think of a better illustration of 2 Peter 3:15-17! Can you?In 1 Corinthians 15, Paul answers the teaching by some "that there is no resurrection of the dead" (verse 12). He does this by first establishing the validity of the bodily resurrection of Jesus Christ (verses 1-11). Then he presents the consequences of denying the resurrection of the dead (verses 12-34). Next, he anticipates objections to bodily resurrection (verses 35-50). Finally, he praises the victory over death God gives us in Christ through the resurrection (verses 51-58). The very thing defined in this chapter is denied by the A.D. 70 doctrine, namely, a future, bodily resurrection! To demonstrate this as the central theme of the chapter, consider verses 20-23. Here the bodily resurrection of all mankind is said to be based upon the bodily resurrection of Christ! The resurrected Christ is the firstfruits of the dead (verses 20, 23). The offering of firstfruits under the Law of Moses was the choicest and earliest ripe crop (Numbers 18:12; Exodus 23:16, 19), indicating that all the crop which followed belonged to God (cf. Deuteronomy 26:2-11). Also, we should note that the crop which followed was of the same kind or type as its firstfruits.

In like manner, the resurrection of Christ from the dead is an assurance and guarantee that all who die shall be raised. And we are assured that our resurrection will be the same kind as His. As surely as bodily death comes to all because of Adam's sin (Genesis 3:19), bodily resurrection will come to all because of Christ's bodily resurrection (verses 21-22). This reveals His power and preeminence over death (cf. John 5:28-29; Colossians 1:18; Revelation 1:18). Thus, Paul defends the doctrine of bodily resurrection from the dead upon the basis of Christ's bodily resurrection. The later fruit (resurrection of all the dead at Christ's coming) must be the same kind of fruit as the firstfruits, namely, bodily resurrection! Jesus' body was raised from the dead, and our bodies shall be raised, too. Nowhere do we discover a Judaism-Christianity contrast in 1 Corinthians 15. That can only be found in the imagination of the A.D. 70 advocates!

The attempt to assign to 70 A.D. every end-time event (including the final coming of Christ, bodily resurrection and the judgment) cannot be supported by Scripture. It is completely refuted by Acts 1:9-11, 2 Peter 3:1-11, and 1 Corinthians 15. But why this fascination with the date of 70 A.D.?

The doctrine which says the personal, second coming of Jesus Christ occurred in 70 A.D. is confusing some brethren and destroying the faith of others. In our previous article, we saw how this doctrine claims that all the second coming prophecies happened in 70 A.D. While showing that Jesus came in judgment against Jerusalem in 70 A.D., we also noticed three passages which teach us that the personal return of Christ is still future. These passages are Acts 1:9-11, 2 Peter 3:4-11, and 1 Corinthians 15. He will come bringing rest to the righteous and punishment to the wicked (2 Thessalonians 1:7-10; Matthew 25:31-46). At His return, all mankind will be resurrected to stand before His judgment-seat, and there receive a just sentence for the deeds done in this life (John 5:28-29; 2 Corinthians 5:10; Revelation 20:12-15). This world shall be dissolved in a fiery judgment, and a new order shall be established (2 Peter 3:10-13). These events did not occur in 70 A.D. It is therefore right to hope for a future return of Jesus Christ. We were not begotten unto a dead hope, but a living one (1 Peter 1:3-5; cf. 1 Corinthians 15:19).

Why has 70 A.D. been made such a focal point in this false doctrine? While several answers could be offered which address this question, I submit that the underlying reason for this doctrinal error rests upon a perverted interpretation of the allegory found in Galatians 4:21-31. In this allegory, the A.D. 70 advocate believes that he finds comfort and support for his doctrine. Instead, he finds a refutation of it!

An Overlapping of the Covenants?

To understand how the allegory of Galatians 4:21-31 fits into the system of Realized Eschatology, consider Max King's following statement:

"Christianity is a fulfillment of the prophecies, types, and shadows of the law and not merely a 'fill-in' between Judaism and another age to come. Abraham had *two* sons, and there was no *gap* between them. They *overlapped* a little, but Isaac 'came on' when Ishmael 'went out.' The son born of the *spirit* was given the place and inheritance of the son born of the *flesh*. Hence, this simple allegory (Galatians 4:21-31) establishes the 'Spirit of Prophecy,' confirming prophecy's fulfillment in the spiritual seed of Abraham through Christ (Galatians 3:16, 26-29), and beyond the fall of Jerusalem these prophecies cannot be extended." (*The Spirit of Prophecy*, Max R. King, page 239. emphasis, King's).

According to King (and others), this allegory establishes his view of the end times. This doctrine teaches that "out of the decay of Judaism arose the spiritual body of Christianity" (*Ibid.*, page 200). We are told that this occurred during the forty year period of 30-70 A.D. Therefore, an overlapping of the old and new covenants is believed to have occurred, and becomes crucial to this doctrine's defense. By having us believe that the old and new covenants overlapped from 30-70 AD., this heresy would have us believe that Christians were "given the place and inheritance" of the Jews. These two allegations (an overlapping of the covenants and Christians being given the inheritance of the Jews) constitute two fatal mistakes in this false doctrine. So then, let us first look at whether or not the old and new covenants overlapped from 30-70 A.D. Then we will consider the inheritance obtained by Christians.

God's word clearly teaches us that the old covenant ceased prior to 70 A.D. To suggest that the covenant remained until 70 A.D. is to deny God's revealed truth. Consider the following evidence:

1) *Romans 7:1-6 - An overlapping of the covenants would amount to spiritual adultery.* It is adultery to be married to another man while one's husband lives (verse 3). With his death, the wife is "discharged from the law of the husband" (verse 2), and is free to marry another (verse 3). With these truths, Paul illustrates man's current relationship to the Law of Moses:

> "...ye also were made dead to the law through the body of Christ; that ye should be joined ("married" - KJV) to another, even to him who was raised from the dead,....But now we have been discharged from the law...." (verses 4, 6).

If the old and new covenants overlapped from 30-70 AD., Paul's illustration would mean nothing! Furthermore, a Jewish Christian would be married to two husbands (covenants) simultaneously, hence, spiritual adultery! More than a decade before 70 A.D., the apostle said, "But now we have been discharged from the law!" There was no overlapping of the covenants!

2) *Colossians 2:13-15 - The focal point in the removal of the old covenant is the cross, not 70 A.D.* In this passage, Paul emphasizes the cross as the means whereby one was released from the "bond written in ordinances." While the old covenant could not forgive (Hebrews 10:1-4), the cross triumphs over sin and its cohorts (verse 15). At the cross, three things regarding the old covenant occurred (verse 14): (1) *It was blotted out.* That is, it was removed, being against or contrary to man's forgiveness. (2) *It was taken out of the way.* Again, its removal is stressed. (3) *It was nailed to the cross.* Triumph over sin occurred at the cross, not 70 A.D.!

3) *2 Corinthians 3:14 - The old covenant is done away in Christ, not in 70 A.D.* Like the Hebrews of Paul's day, the A.D. 70 advocate fails to perceive that the old covenant was done away in Christ. The old covenant was already done away when Paul wrote this passage! Only minds "hardened" to this truth could miss the apostle's meaning.

4) *Hebrews 7:11-14 - An overlapping of the covenants would mean two priesthoods were in force at the same time.* Under the old covenant, the Levitical priesthood was in force (verse 11). However, Christ is not a priest

like Aaron (verse 11), but one who is "after the likeness of Melchizedek" (verses 15, 3). Because Jesus came from the tribe of Judah and not Levi, He could not serve as a priest while the old law was in force (verses 13-14; Hebrews 8:4). The law had to change to enable Jesus Christ to serve as priest over the house of God (Hebrews 7:12, 15-17; 10:21; 3:1; 5:5-6; 6:20). Jesus did not wait until 70 A.D. to become a priest. Neither did He gradually become one. He began serving as High Priest when He sat down at God's right hand (Hebrews 8:1-2). Therefore, since Jesus served as High Priest before 70 A.D., the law was changed before 70 A.D. (Hebrews 7:12).

5) *Ephesians 2:13-18 - Christ made peace between Jews and Gentiles in His death, not in 70 A.D.* Again, we find the Bible teaching us that the cross is the focal point of God's plan for peace and human redemption, not 70 A.D. "He is our peace" (verse 13), thus identifying Christ as the one who accomplished peace between Jews and Gentiles. When and how did He do this? He produced peace between Jews and Gentiles by removing that which stood as a barrier between them, namely, the "law of commandments contained in ordinances" (verses 14-15). This abolition of the "middle wall of partition," with its enmity, occurred "in his flesh" (verse 15). Verse 16 confirms this as Christ's death, by teaching us that reconciliation with God was accomplished "through the cross, having slain the enmity thereby." Peace between the Jews and Gentiles, and reconciliation with God, was not achieved only after a 40-year struggle of the two covenants (with the new one finally overcoming the old one!). Salvation by grace through faith (Ephesians 2:8) was available for all flesh, and preached without distinction to all flesh, long before 70 A.D. (Acts 2:17, 21, 39; 11:12-18; 10:34-35; 15:7-11). Access to God for both Jews and Gentiles is through Christ's death (verse 18).

Were Christians Given the Place and Inheritance of the Jews?

Realized Eschatology would have you believe that Christians were given the place and inheritance of the Jews. Recall Max King's quote, given earlier, where he said, "They *overlapped* a little, but Isaac 'came on' when Ishmael 'went out.' The son born of the *spirit* was given the place and inheritance of the son born of the *flesh*" (The Spirit of Prophecy, page 239). By redefining the allegory of Galatians 4:21-31, the A.D. 70 doctrine has occasioned its own downfall.

An assumed purpose of Paul's allegory is used as the basis for contending that Christians were given the place and inheritance of the Jews:

The purpose of Paul in this allegory was threefold: First, *to show that Abraham had two sons which existed side by side* for a time in the same household. This is a truth that is vital to the teachings of the New Testament, and will be a key factor in the study and application of prophecy. Much misapplication of scripture can be attributed to a failure to recognize this simple but vital truth. These two sons are typical of the two Israels of God, one born after the flesh (old covenant) and the other born after the Spirit (new covenant)....*Ishmael was the first born and, as such, had the right of primogeniture, a right he maintained at the birth of Isaac, and even thereafter UNTIL he was cast out or disinherited"* (Ibid., pages 29-30, emphasis mine, jrp).

Realized Eschatology's redefinition of the allegory concludes that Ishmael was the rightful heir of Abraham "UNTIL" he was "cast out." Thus, we should believe that the Jews under the old covenant were the rightful heirs of the inheritance, but were "cast out" at 70 A.D. (at which time Christians took their place and received the Jews' inheritance). However, the Bible declares that Ishmael was never heir of the Abrahamic promises (Genesis 12:1-3)! Remember, Ishmael was Sarah's remedy for Abraham's lack of an heir (inasmuch as she gave her handmaid Hagar to Abraham, Genesis 16.1-3), not God's. Even before Isaac was born, God made it clear that Ishmael was not heir of the promises He had made, when He declared that His covenant would be established with Isaac, not Ishmael (Genesis 17:15-21). Since Ishmael never was heir to these blessings, he could not be "disinherited" of them! Isaac did not take Ishmael's place as heir! Neither did Christians take the Jews' place as heirs of God's inheritance!

The old covenant did not contain the inheritance of God's Abrahamic promises. Righteousness and justification is not through the law, but through faith in Christ (Galatians 2:16, 21; 3:7-14, 21-23; Romans 3:20-22). The law gave a knowledge of sin (Romans 3:20), but no release from it (Galatians 3:10, 12, 22-23). It produced "children of bondage" (Galatians 4:24). It contained no inheritance (Galatians 3:18-19), only a curse (Galatians 3:10-14). The "righteousness of God through faith in Jesus Christ" (Romans 3:22) is "apart from the law" (Romans 3:21). Therefore, the "children of promise" (Galatians 4:28 - Christians) did not receive their inheritance from the Jews of the old covenant. If they did, the inheritance would be "no more of promise" (Galatians 3:18). To suggest that Christians were given the place and inheritance of the Jews is to demonstrate a woeful misunderstanding of God's promise to Abraham and how it is received. Its blessings are received through faith in Jesus Christ (Galatians 3:16-19, 23-29), not through the law. Our inheritance is "according to promise," not according to the law!

The Allegory of Galatians 4:21-31 Denies the A.D. 70 Doctrine

Max King's quote from page 239 of his book says "this simple allegory (Gal. 4:21-31) establishes the 'Spirit of prophecy.'" Instead, the truth of this allegory destroys the A.D. 70 doctrine. Why was this allegory used by the apostle Paul? What does the allegory teach?

The background of the allegory is found in Galatians 3:23-29, where the inspired teacher makes four needed observations:

1) Verse 23 - The law of Moses was in force, and men were under it, BEFORE faith came.

2) Verses 24-25 - The law was a tutor to bring men to Christ, and now that tutor was no longer needed.

3) Verse 25 - Paul says "NOW" faith is here (59-60 A.D.).

4) Verses 26-29 - We are children of God and heirs according to promise through faith in Christ, not through the Law of Moses.

Having used Galatians 3 to teach that Christians are not justified by the law of Moses, but through faith in Christ, Paul now addresses those Christians who "desire to be under the law" (Galatians 4:21), and shows them that the law itself contains an illustration of how their desire was out of place.

The allegory (Galatians 4:21-31) uses Sarah and Hagar as the two covenants (verse 24), and their sons as the product of those covenants. Hagar signifies the Mosaic Law, which produced "children of bondage" (verse 24). Verse 25 emphasizes this point of bondage (cf. Galatians 3:10, 22; Romans 3:20). Sarah corresponds to the new covenant. Isaac corresponds to Christians, who are the children of promise (verses 26-28). In verse 29, the children of bondage (Jews) are presented as persecutors of the children of promise (Christians), just as Ishmael was the persecutor of Isaac (not "the firstborn" of Abraham). What should Christians do? Should they desire to be under the law? Should they turn back to bondage by joining their persecutors? NO! The allegory teaches them (and us) to not go back to the law and live under it, for that would place them (and us) in the bondage of sin. Instead, "cast out the handmaid (old covenant) and her son (Jews with their persecutions)," and live in the freedom of the new covenant (Galatians 4:30-5:4). God says to purge yourself from turning back to the Mosaic Law, and to live as the children of promise that you are! Do not live in bondage to the law and its curse, but in freedom from sin and death through faith in Christ!

The allegory does not carry within it the arbitrary definitions and subjective applications which the A.D. 70 doctrine places upon it. We cannot apply the allegory beyond where and how the inspired apostle of Christ applied it. To make of it an "embryonic statement" of the Realized Eschatology theory is a wresting of Scripture (2 Peter 3:16) by the wisdom of men (1 Corinthians 3:18-20; Romans 1:22).

Such mishandling of the word of truth must be avoided (2 Timothy 2:15) and contended against (Jude 3-4). In our final installment on the A.D. 70 doctrine, we will look at some of the grave consequences of its principle tenets

The proponents of Realized Eschatology, or the "A.D. 70" doctrine, have deceived and are deceiving some brethren into believing that all the end time events have already been accomplished. Its advocates have caused unsuspecting Christians to accept the belief that the events of 70 A.D. in the destruction of Jerusalem satisfy all the prophecies of a future return of Christ, resurrection of the dead, judgment and reception of the eternal inheritance. It would have us believe that the "last days" existed from 30-70 A.D., and that the "eternal days" began at 70 A.D. We are supposedly living in the "eternal days!" The "Bible" of this doctrine, Max King's *The Spirit of Prophecy*, has this to say on page 81: "...whenever faulty interpretation creates a time period that doesn't exist in the Bible, more error will follow by attributing to that period something that cannot belong to it." I say AMEN to that!

This 40-year "gap" where the old and new covenants supposedly "overlapped" is the result of faulty interpretation, and it has borne its evil fruit! (See Part II of this series for more information on the overlapping of the covenants.)

Simply stated, the A.D. 70 doctrine has the following things being accomplished on that date:

1) Second coming of Christ (as per 1 Corinthians 15:23).

2) Resurrection of the dead (as per 1 Corinthians 15).

3) Judgment / Day of the Lord (as per 2 Peter 3:10; et al.).

4) Establishment of the new covenant.

5) Completeness in Christ (adulthood, adoption, redemption).

6) Kingdom fully established.

7) Reception of the eternal inheritance.

To document these positions as central to this doctrine, consider this assessment from the pen of Max King:

> The fall of Judaism (and its far reaching consequences) is, therefore, a *major* (emp., King's) subject of the Bible. The greater portion of prophecy found its fulfillment in that event, including also the types and shadows of the law. It was the coming of Christ in glory that closely followed his coming in suffering (1 Pet. 1:11), when all things written by the prophets were fulfilled (Luke 21:22; Acts 3:21). It corresponded to the *perfection of the saints (1 Cor. 13:10) when the reached adulthood in Christ, receiving their adoption, redemption, and inheritance. The eternal kingdom was possessed (Heb. 12:28) and the new heaven and earth inherited (Matt. 5:5; Rev. 21:1, 7)"* - The Spirit of Prophecy, p. 239; emp. jrp).

In Part I of this series, we addressed the major problems of this doctrine by looking at what the New Testament has to say about the second coming of Christ (including the judgment and the resurrection of the dead). In Part II, we discussed why 70 A.D. is made such a focal point in this system of error, with emphasis upon the old and new covenants and the allegory of Galatians 4:21-31. In this final article, we must consider some of the consequences of this doctrine, and see that it is not a harmless, private conviction which can be held without hurting oneself and others, but a pernicious theory of error which engulfs the souls of men in destructive heresy! Given this doctrine's premise that God's scheme of redemption was *not complete until 70 A.D.,* there are some very grave consequences which necessarily follow.

Problems Regarding Resurrection

1) *Luke 20:34-36 - No marriage and no death after 70 A.D.!* This consequence centers upon the view that the "last days" are to be defined as the closing period of the Jewish age, 30 - 70 A.D., with the "eternal days" continuing from that point. "We are *now* in that world 'which is to come' ....instead of being in *last days* we are in *eternal days* world without end (Ephesians 3:21)." (Ibid., page 81; emphasis King's). So, in the New Testament, those who lived between 30-70 A.D. were in the "last days," while we now live in the "eternal days." However, in Luke 20:34-36, Jesus contrasts "this world" and "that world" following the resurrection of the dead, and concludes that while marriage occurs in "this world," it will not be so in "that world." Plus, those who "are accounted worthy to attain to *that world*, and the resurrection of the dead,...die no more" (verses 35-36). Are people still marrying after 70 A.D.?! Of course they are! Are they still dying? Most certainly! Is the period of Christianity in which we now live termed the "eternal days" in the New Testament? No! Otherwise, following 70 A.D., Christians would be prohibited from marrying, and neither could they die anymore! The A.D. 70 doctrine is false!

2) *Acts 24:15 - The Pharisees and Paul looked for the same kind of resurrection.* Here it must be remembered that the A.D. 70 doctrine holds that the resurrection of the dead discussed in such places as 1 Corinthians 15 is the resurrection of Christianity out of Judaism (*The Spirit of Prophecy*, page 200). But if this is the truth of the matter, then the Pharisees held a very strange hope concerning the resurrection! Paul states that his accusers before Felix were looking for "a resurrection both of the just and unjust," the same as Paul. Must we conclude these Jewish accusers were looking forward to the day when Christianity would arise to dominance, while Judaism would be destroyed under God's wrath?! Surely this is not what they were "looking for" (verse 15; John 11:48-50), but we are told they were looking for the same resurrection Paul hoped for. Maybe the apostle Paul was wrong in his assessment of the Jews' hope, or maybe the A.D. 70 doctrine is wrong in its assessment of the resurrection of the dead! What do you think?

3) *1 Corinthians 15:20-23 - The bodily resurrection of Jesus is called into doubt by this doctrine.* Christ is presented as the "firstfruits" (verse 20) of the dead, which identifies Him as the beginning and the guarantor of a future, *bodily* resurrection (verses 21-22, 35-49). The resurrection of the dead endorsed by 1 Corinthians 15 is a future, *bodily* resurrection of

mankind, based upon the *fact* of Christ's *bodily* resurrection. If, however, the *body* to be raised in 1 Corinthians 15 is "Christianity out of Judaism," why must we believe in the *bodily* resurrection of Christ? If the later fruit resurrection of the dead - verse 21) is not the *bodily* resurrection of mankind, there is no real reason to believe the "firstfruits" (verses 20, 23) was the *bodily* resurrection of Christ! (The firstfruits and the later fruits must be the same type of fruit!) The whole issue of Jesus' *bodily* resurrection is called into doubt, and is a logical consequence of this doctrine. Are the proponents of the A.D. 70 doctrine ready to accept this consequence of their doctrine? If one will not accept the consequences of his position, he should renounce his position as the error that it is!

These are but three consequences regarding resurrection from the dead which logically result from the A.D. 70 doctrine. Like the error of Hymenaeus and Philetus (who said the resurrection is past already, 2 Timothy 2:16-18), the A.D. 70 doctrine "proceed(s) further in ungodliness," as it eats like a cankerous sore upon the souls of men, spreading its decay and overthrowing the faith of saints. The plea of this writer is that those who currently hold to this doctrine will see its destructive effects upon "the faith of some" (verse 18), and renounce their acceptance of it.

Problems Regarding Human Redemption

1) *Forgiveness of sins was not fully accomplished until 70 A.D. Forgiveness of sins was not fully accomplished until 70 A.D.* This doctrine does not regard forgiveness of sins as an accomplished fact until 70 A.D. "*When* would ungodliness be turned away from Jacob, or their sins be taken away? When Christ, the deliverer, came OUT OF ZION. *When* did Christ come out of Zion? Not at his first coming, but his *second coming*" (The Spirit of Prophecy, page 63; emphasis, King's). The cross of Christ is thus removed as the focal point and means of accomplishing forgiveness, and replaced by 70 A.D.! Such a consequence reduces the Scriptures to shambles, and makes deceptive the many appeals to people *before* 70 A.D. to receive the forgiveness of their sins through the death of Christ. In Acts 2:38, the apostle said "Repent ye, and be baptized every one of you in the name of Jesus Christ unto *the remission of your sins*; and ye shall receive the gift of the Holy Spirit." This Jewish audience did not have to wait until 70 A.D. to have their sins remitted! Acts 22:16 gives instruction to Saul to *"wash away thy sins."* by being baptized. Baptism puts one into the death of Christ (Romans 6:3), to enable justification by His blood (Romans 5:8-9). Forgiveness of sins was accomplished by the cross of Christ! In Romans 6:17-18, when the Romans "became obedient from the heart"

to the gospel, they were *"made free from sin,"* and "became servants of righteousness." This happened long before 70 A.D.!

Referring back to the quote at the start of this article from page 239 of The Spirit of Prophecy, notice that Realized Eschatology says that our *adoption, redemption* and *inheritance* were accomplished at the fall of Judaism (70 A.D.). Yet Galatians 4:3-7 places the means of our *adoption* at the first coming of Christ (verses 4-5), and its reality prior to 70 A.D., when Paul says "ye are sons" (verse 6). Our *redemption* was accomplished at the cross (Galatians 3:13-14; Hebrews 9:11-12). Our *inheritance* as sons of God is thereby assured (Romans 8:16-17; Galatians 3:18). Forgiveness and its blessings are ours today because of the cross of Christ, not because of the fall of Judaism in 70 A.D.

2) *Maturity or completeness in Christ was not possible before 70 A.D.* So implies King's quote from page 239 of his book. However, Colossians 2:10 says "in him ye *are* made full." In chapter 1:27-28, Christ was being proclaimed 'that we may present every man *perfect in Christ*." They were not proclaiming the fall of Judaism in 70 A.D. as the means of perfection (completeness, full growth, maturity)! This doctrine concludes that no Christian could be mature in Christ before 70 A.D.—not apostles, not elders, not any child of God! The ramifications of that consequence are mind-boggling.

Problems Regarding the Establishment of the Kingdom

By misapplying Hebrews 12:28, this doctrine concludes that the kingdom was not *fully* established until 70 A.D. However, we again find this doctrine at odds with revealed truth. In Isaiah 2:2, it was prophesied "And it shall come to pass in the latter days, that the mountain of Lord's house *shall be established* on the top of the mountains, and *shall be exalted* above the hills; and all nations shall flow unto it." Realized Eschatology would have God's house or kingdom only *partially* established in the "latter days," and only *fully* established at 70 A.D., their "eternal days." Isaiah implies full and complete establishment in verse 2, and reveals this would occur when the law and the word of Jehovah would go forth from Jerusalem (verse 3). The gospel of the kingdom was preached from Jerusalem unto all the nations following Jesus ascension (Luke 24:45-49; Acts 1:5; 2:14-36). Therefore, the kingdom predicted by Isaiah was established as he said it would be, on the day of Pentecost (Acts 2).

Jesus said the kingdom would "come with power," and that some of His disciples would not taste of death until they saw it come (Mark 9:1). The

Realized Eschatology

"power" referred to must be the heavenly power of Holy Spirit baptism, received by the apostles on the day of Pentecost (Luke 24:49; Acts 1:4-5, 8; 2:1-4, 33). There is no hint in the Scriptures that this was only *partial* power, or that the kingdom and its blessings were only *partially* present! Full power and full blessings amounted to a *fully established kingdom* on the day of Pentecost! What parts were missing? Its king (Luke 1:32-33; 1 Timothy 1:17; 6:15)? Its territory (Mark 16:15)? Its subjects (Acts 10:34-35)? Its law (Mark 16:15; James 1:25)? People did not have to wait until 70 A.D. to fully possess the kingdom! They were being translated into the kingdom (Colossians 1:13) from Pentecost onward. To deny the full establishment of the kingdom before 70 A.D. is to deny the fullness of its king (Jesus), its gospel (power to save, Romans 1:16), and its blessings (Ephesians 1:3-4) before 70 A.D.! This is untenable and blasphemous!

Problems Regarding Worship

1) *Should the Lord's Supper be observed after 70 A.D.?* According to 1 Corinthians 11:26, in partaking of the Lord's Supper we "proclaim the Lord's death till he come." Since the A.D. 70 doctrine makes every coming of the Lord in the New Testament mean 70 A.D., we wonder, what are its advocates going to do about the Lord's Supper? There are two options open to them, and both are equally unacceptable. First, they could conclude that after 70 A.D. the Lord's Supper no longer proclaims Christ's death. But this destroys the central meaning and effect of the Supper! Secondly, they could conclude that the Lord's Supper is no longer applicable to Christians and cease partaking of it. Some Christians are currently wrestling with this consequence of their doctrine. Either horn of this dilemma is sharp and will cause pain and great damage to the one who attempts to set upon it. Which shall it be? Instead, why not renounce this system of error which places such devastating consequences upon the Christian's observance of the Lord's Supper?!

2) *One must eliminate from his worship every hymn and spiritual song referring to the return of Jesus Christ and its events.* I have witnessed Christians not singing with their brethren (Ephesians 5:19; Colossians 3:16) because of this consequence! Why sing about something you believe has already occurred? Are you willing to renounce your brethren as guilty of false worship whenever they sing about the future return of Christ and its events? And to be consistent in your worship, you will have to make that choice about the Lord's Supper. Will you eliminate it, or destroy its meaning?!

These consequences should be weighed in the light of God's revelation of truth. Realized Eschatology opens a can of worms that some brethren have not realized. Some may try to ignore its consequences, but this will only lead to hardened hearts. To accept these consequences will steep a person deeper in error and apostasy. God's remedy is still available—repentance of this sinful doctrine (Acts 8:22), confession of the sin (1 John 1:9), and doing works worthy of repentance (Acts 26:20; Luke3:8) by renouncing this doctrine of man.

Comforting Christians Concerning Christ's Coming

1 Thessalonians 4:13-18 provides us a fitting conclusion to this series of articles. In this passage, the apostle comforts the saints with assurance that Christians who die before Jesus returns will not miss out on any of the events and blessings of that grand day. He contrasts living and dead Christians throughout this passage—alien sinners are not in view here. Jesus "himself" will descend from heaven (this did not happen in 70 A.D.). Audible and visible events will occur. A "shout" commanding death to give up its prisoners will go forth (John 5:28-29). The "voice of the archangel" will herald the power and victory of Christ's return (cf. 2 Thessalonians 1:7). The "trump of God" shall sound, signaling deliverance and liberty from death (cf. 1 Corinthians 15:52; Leviticus 25:9-10). These things did not happen in 70 A.D. The dead in Christ shall rise first, with the living Christians being "caught up in the clouds," and all the saints shall "meet the Lord in the air" (this did not happen in 70 A.D.). Then "so shall we ever be with the Lord." We will ever be with the Lord in this resurrected, changed, caught-up state (this did not happen in 70 A.D.)! We can comfort one another with these words (verse 18), but there is surely no comfort in the words and doctrines of Realized Eschatology. It provides no final and decisive solution to the sin problem humanity faces. It presents a world in sin which will forever continue. The Bible reveals that with the Lord's personal return (Acts 1:9-11), this sin-cursed world will be destroyed (2 Peter 3:5-12), with a new order taking its place (2 Peter 3:13).

In view of these realities, Christians should be comforted in their hope of the future return of Christ (1 Thessalonians 4:18; 2 Thessalonians 1:10; Colossians 3:4). But sinners and perverters of God's word should convert to Christ, for it will *certainly be "a fearful thing to fall into the hands of the living God"(Hebrews 10:31; 2 Thessalonians 1:7-9*[11]

---

[11] Joe R. Price

CHAPTER 8
Haunting Questions Regarding Realized Eschatology and the A. D. 70 Doctrine

Introduction

Realized Eschatology affirms that all prophecies regarding "the end times" were fulfilled in A.D. 70 at the destruction of Jerusalem, including: The Second Coming of Christ, The Resurrection of the Dead, The Day of Judgment, The End of the World, etc.[12]

Furthermore, proponents of this doctrine affirm that Christ's Kingdom/Church was not fully established on Pentecost. Instead, the kingdom was born in Acts 2, but did not come with "power" and fullness until Jerusalem was destroyed in A. D. 70. "The last days" never apply to the Christian Age, but always to the closing period of the Jewish Age (A.D. 30 - A.D. 70).

One principle of biblical interpretation is the law of harmony: Truth is consistent with itself (Psalm 119:160). We should examine all that the Bible says on a given subject, and not interpret one passage so as to contradict another. However, when the artificial grid of the A.D. 70 doctrine is imposed upon Scripture, all manner of problems are created. In this lesson, let us consider some of the haunting questions that arise when the four-square gospel is forced into the circular reasoning of Realized Eschatology.

> Psalm 119:160 ... ¹⁶⁰the sum of Your word is truth, And every one of Your righteous ordinances is everlasting. (NASB)

The End of the Age

The expression "end of the age(s)" occurs 7x in the Bible (Daniel 12:13;

---

[12] Sermon by Mark Mayberry, July 12, 2009, in Conroe, Texas, used by permission

Matthew 13:39, 40, 49; 24:3; 28:20; 1 Corinthians 10:11). Meaning is determined by context, with certain passages having an application that was near at hand (1 Corinthians 10:11; Matthew 24:3), and others referring to the far distant future (Daniel 12:13; Matthew 13:39, 40, 49, 20).

> *Daniel 12:13 - "But as for you, go your way to the end; then you will enter into rest and rise again for your allotted portion at the end of the age." (NASB)*

> *Matthew 13:39 - and the enemy who sowed them is the devil, and the harvest is the end of the age; and the reapers are angels. (NASB)*

> *Matthew 13:40 - "So just as the tares are gathered up and burned with fire, so shall it be at the end of the age. (NASB)*

> *Matthew 13:49 - "So it will be at the end of the age; the angels will come forth and take out the wicked from among the righteous, (NASB)*

> *Matthew 24:3 - As He was sitting on the Mount of Olives, the disciples came to Him privately, saying, "Tell us, when will these things happen, and what will be the sign of Your coming, and of the end of the age?" (NASB)*

> *Matthew 28:20 - teaching them to observe all that I commanded you; and lo, I am with you always, even to the end of the age." (NASB)*

> *1 Corinthians 10:11 - Now these things happened to them as an example, and they were written for our instruction, upon whom the ends of the ages have come. (NASB)*

If the end of the age occurred in 70 A.D., why is Daniel not among us (Daniel 12:13)?

> *Daniel 12:13 - "But as for you, go your way to the end; then you will enter into rest and rise again for your allotted portion at the end of the age." (NASB)*

If the end of the age occurred 70 A.D, why are the wicked still among us (Matthew 13:36-43)?

> *Matthew 13:36-43 - ³⁶Then He left the crowds and went into the house. And His disciples came to Him and said, "Explain to us the parable of the tares of the field." ³⁷And He said, "The one who sows the good seed is the Son of Man, ³⁸and the field is the world; and as for the good seed, these are the sons of the kingdom; and the tares are the sons of the evil one; ³⁹and the enemy who sowed them is the devil, and the harvest is the end of the age; and the reapers are angels. ⁴⁰"So just as the tares are gathered up and burned with fire, so shall it be at the end of the age. ⁴¹"The Son of Man will send forth His angels, and they will gather out of His kingdom all stumbling blocks, and those who commit lawlessness, ⁴²and will throw them into the furnace of fire; in that place there will be weeping and gnashing of teeth. ⁴³"Then the righteous will shine forth as the sun in the kingdom of their Father. He who has ears, let him hear. (NASB)*

If the end of the age occurred in 70 A.D., by what authority do we preach the gospel (Matthew 28:18-20)?

> *Matthew 28:18-20 - ¹⁸And Jesus came up and spoke to them, saying, "All authority has been given to Me in heaven and on earth. ¹⁹"Go therefore and make disciples of all the nations, baptizing them in the name of the Father and the Son and the Holy Spirit, ²⁰teaching them to observe all that I commanded you; and lo, I am with you always, even to **the end of the age**." (NASB)*

The Lord's Coming

In the Old Testament "the coming of the Lord" was used prophetically of God's judgment upon the nations, and of the coming of the Messiah. In the New Testament, it has various meanings. He Came/ He Has Come refers to the physical incarnation of Jesus Christ, His earthly ministry, and the establishment of the church on Pentecost. He comes in judgment upon individuals, (Herod), churches (Ephesus, Pergamum, Philadelphia) and upon cities and nations (Jerusalem and the nation of Israel, Rome and the Roman Empire). He Will Come/He Is Coming also refers to the Second Coming of Jesus Christ.

If the Lord's coming occurred in 70 A.D., what is so remarkable about Jesus' statement to Peter (John 21:20-23)?

> *John 21:20-23 - [20]Peter, turning around, saw the disciple whom Jesus loved following them; the one who also had leaned back on His bosom at the supper and said, "Lord, who is the one who betrays You?" [21]So Peter seeing him said to Jesus, "Lord, and what about this man?" [22]Jesus said to him, "If I want him to remain until I come, what is that to you? You follow Me!" [23]Therefore this saying went out among the brethren that that disciple would not die; yet Jesus did not say to him that he would not die, but only, "If I want him to remain until I come, what is that to you?" (NASB)*

If the Lord's coming occurred in 70 A.D., why can we not judge the hidden things of the heart (1 Corinthians 4:1-5)?

> *1 Corinthians 4:1-5 - [1] Let a man regard us in this manner, as servants of Christ and stewards of the mysteries of God. [2] In this case, moreover, it is required of stewards that one be found trustworthy. [3]But to me it is a very small thing that I may be examined by you, or by any human court; in fact, I do not even examine myself. [4] For I am conscious of nothing against myself, yet I am not by this acquitted; but the one who examines me is the Lord. [5]Therefore do not go on passing judgment before the time, but wait until the Lord comes who will both bring to light the things hidden in the darkness and disclose the motives of men's hearts; and then each man's praise will come to him from God. (NASB)*

If the Lord's coming occurred in 70 A.D., why do we still observe the Lord's Supper (1 Corinthians 11:23-26)?

> *1 Corinthians 11:23-26 -* [23]*For I received from the Lord that which I also delivered to you, that the Lord Jesus in the night in which He was betrayed took bread;* [24]*and when He had given thanks, He broke it and said, "This is My body, which is for you; do this in remembrance of Me."* [25]*In the same way He took the cup also after supper, saying, "This cup is the new covenant in My blood; do this, as often as you drink it, in remembrance of Me."* [26]*For as often as you eat this bread and drink the cup, you proclaim the Lord's death until He comes. (NASB)*

The Resurrection

The resurrection concept is communicated by the Greek word *anastasis*, derived from *anistēmi* [to raise up, to rise], which identifies "a standing up, i.e. a resurrection, a raising up, rising" [Thomas 386].

BDAG say it can refer to either (1) a change for the better in status, rising up, rise (Luke 2:34); (2) resurrection from the dead, resurrection; (a) in the past: of Jesus' resurrection (Acts 4:33; etc.); (b) of the future resurrection, linked with Judgment Day (Acts 24:15; etc.).

> *Luke 2:34 - And Simeon blessed them and said to Mary His mother, "Behold, this Child is appointed for the fall and **rise** of many in Israel, and for a sign to be opposed— (NASB)*

> *Acts 4:33 - And with great power the apostles were giving testimony to the **resurrection** of the Lord Jesus, and abundant grace was upon them all. (NASB)*

> *Acts 24:15 - having a hope in God, which these men cherish themselves, that there shall certainly be a **resurrection** of both the righteous and the wicked. (NASB)*

This word is never used symbolically in reference to the resurrection of a cause. Note the popularity of liberal views regarding the resurrection. Max King takes a similar approach in saying that the church arose out of the ruins of Judaism.

If the resurrection occurred in 70 A.D., why is there still marriage (Matthew 22:23-33)?

> *Matthew 22:23-33 - [23]On that day some Sadducees (who say there is no resurrection) came to Jesus and questioned Him, [24]asking, "Teacher, Moses said, 'If a man dies having no children, his brother as next of kin shall marry his wife, and raise up children for his brother.' [25]"Now there were seven brothers with us; and the first married and died, and having no children left his wife to his brother; [26]so also the second, and the third, down to the seventh. [27]"Last of all, the woman died. [28]"In the resurrection, therefore, whose wife of the seven will she be? For they all had married her." [29]But Jesus answered and said to them, "You are mistaken, not understanding the Scriptures nor the power of God. [30]"For in the resurrection they neither marry nor are given in marriage, but are like angels in heaven. [31]"But regarding the resurrection of the dead, have you not read what was spoken to you by God: [32]'I am the God of Abraham, and the God of Isaac, and the God of Jacob'? He is not the God of the dead but of the living." [33]When the crowds heard this, they were astonished at His teaching. (NASB)*

If the resurrection occurred in 70 A.D., why is there still death (Luke 20:27-40)?

> *Luke 20:27-40 - [27]Now there came to Him some of the Sadducees (who say that there is no resurrection), [28]and they questioned Him, saying, "Teacher, Moses wrote for us that if a man's brother dies, having a wife, and he is childless, his brother should marry the wife and raise up children to his brother. [29]"Now there were seven brothers; and the first took*

a wife and died childless; ^{30}*and the second* ^{31}*and the third married her; and in the same way all seven died, leaving no children.* ^{32}*"Finally the woman died also.* ^{33}*"In the resurrection therefore, which one's wife will she be? For all seven had married her."* ^{34}*Jesus said to them, "The sons of this age marry and are given in marriage,* ^{35}*but those who are considered worthy to attain to that age and the resurrection from the dead, neither marry nor are given in marriage;* ^{36}*for they cannot even die anymore, because they are like angels, and are sons of God, being sons of the resurrection.* ^{37}*"But that the dead are raised, even Moses showed, in the passage about the burning bush, where he calls the Lord the God of Abraham, and the God of Isaac, and the God of Jacob.* ^{38}*"Now He is not the God of the dead but of the living; for all live to Him."* ^{39}*Some of the scribes answered and said, "Teacher, You have spoken well."* ^{40}*For they did not have courage to question Him any longer about anything. (NASB)*

If the resurrection occurred in 70 A.D., when will the righteous be repaid (Luke 14:12-14)?

Luke 14:12-14 - ^{12}*And He also went on to say to the one who had invited Him, "When you give a luncheon or a dinner, do not invite your friends or your brothers or your relatives or rich neighbors, otherwise they may also invite you in return and that will be your repayment.* ^{13}*"But when you give a reception, invite the poor, the crippled, the lame, the blind,* ^{14}*and you will be blessed, since they do not have the means to repay you; for you will be repaid at the resurrection of the righteous." (NASB)*

If the resurrection occurred in 70 A.D., what is the resurrection of the wicked (John 5:28-29; Acts 24:14-15)?

John 5:28-29 - ^{28}*"Do not marvel at this; for an hour is coming, in which all who are in the tombs will hear His voice,* ^{29}*and will come forth; those who did the good deeds to a resurrection of life, those who committed the evil deeds to a resurrection of judgment. (NASB)*

Acts 24:14-15 - ¹⁴"But this I admit to you, that according to the Way which they call a sect I do serve the God of our fathers, believing everything that is in accordance with the Law and that is written in the Prophets; ¹⁵having a hope in God, which these men cherish themselves, that there shall certainly be a resurrection of both the righteous and the wicked. (NASB)

If the resurrection is merely symbolic, why did the Athenians scoff (Acts 17:16-18, 30-32)?

Acts 17:16-18 - ¹⁶Now while Paul was waiting for them at Athens, his spirit was being provoked within him as he was observing the city full of idols. ¹⁷So he was reasoning in the synagogue with the Jews and the God-fearing Gentiles, and in the market place every day with those who happened to be present. ¹⁸And also some of the Epicurean and Stoic philosophers were conversing with him. Some were saying, "What would this idle babbler wish to say?" Others, "He seems to be a proclaimer of strange deities,"—because he was preaching Jesus and the resurrection. (NASB)

Acts 17:30-32 - ³⁰"Therefore having overlooked the times of ignorance, God is now declaring to men that all people everywhere should repent, ³¹because He has fixed a day in which He will judge the world in righteousness through a Man whom He has appointed, having furnished proof to all men by raising Him from the dead." ³²Now when they heard of the resurrection of the dead, some began to sneer, but others said, "We shall hear you again concerning this." (NASB)

If the resurrection is merely symbolic, why did Paul so closely identify himself with the Pharisees, who believed in a literal

resurrection (Acts 23:6-10; 24:20-21)?

> *Acts 23:6-10 - ⁶But perceiving that one group were Sadducees and the other Pharisees, Paul began crying out in the Council, "Brethren, I am a Pharisee, a son of Pharisees; I am on trial for the hope and resurrection of the dead!" ⁷As he said this, there occurred a dissension between the Pharisees and Sadducees, and the assembly was divided. ⁸For the Sadducees say that there is no resurrection, nor an angel, nor a spirit, but the Pharisees acknowledge them all. ⁹And there occurred a great uproar; and some of the scribes of the Pharisaic party stood up and began to argue heatedly, saying, "We find nothing wrong with this man; suppose a spirit or an angel has spoken to him?" ¹⁰And as a great dissension was developing, the commander was afraid Paul would be torn to pieces by them and ordered the troops to go down and take him away from them by force, and bring him into the barracks. (NASB)*

> *Acts 24:20-21 - ²⁰"Or else let these men themselves tell what misdeed they found when I stood before the Council, ²¹other than for this one statement which I shouted out while standing among them, 'For the resurrection of the dead I am on trial before you today.'" (NASB)*

If the resurrection occurred in 70 A.D., what is there left for us to attain (Philippians 3:7-11)?

> *Philippians 3:7-11 - ⁷But whatever things were gain to me, those things I have counted as loss for the sake of Christ. ⁸More than that, I count all things to be loss in view of the surpassing value of knowing Christ Jesus my Lord, for whom I have suffered the loss of all things, and count them but rubbish so that I may gain Christ, ⁹and may be found in Him, not having a righteousness of my own derived from the Law, but that which is through faith in Christ, the righteousness which comes from God on the basis of faith, ¹⁰that I may know Him and the power of His resurrection and the fellowship of*

His sufferings, being conformed to His death; ¹¹in order that I may attain to the resurrection from the dead. (NASB)

If the resurrection is already past, why do we practice baptism (Romans 6:4-11; 1 Corinthians 15:29; 1 Peter 3:21-22)?

Romans 6:4-11 - ⁴Therefore we have been buried with Him through baptism into death, so that as Christ was raised from the dead through the glory of the Father, so we too might walk in newness of life. ⁵For if we have become united with Him in the likeness of His death, certainly we shall also be in [the likeness of] His resurrection, 6knowing this, that our old self was crucified with Him, in order that our body of sin might be done away with, so that we would no longer be slaves to sin; ⁷for he who has died is freed from sin. ⁸Now if we have died with Christ, we believe that we shall also live with Him, ⁹knowing that Christ, having been raised from the dead, is never to die again; death no longer is master over Him. ¹⁰For the death that He died, He died to sin once for all; but the life that He lives, He lives to God. ¹¹Even so consider yourselves to be dead to sin, but alive to God in Christ Jesus. (NASB)

1 Corinthians 15:29 - Otherwise, what will those do who are baptized for the dead? If the dead are not raised at all, why then are they baptized for them? (NASB)

1 Peter 3:21-22 - ²¹Corresponding to that, baptism now saves you—not the removal of dirt from the flesh, but an appeal to God for a good conscience—through the resurrection of Jesus Christ, ²²who is at the right hand of God, having gone into heaven, after angels and authorities and powers had been subjected to Him. (NASB)

Conclusion

How is the doctrine of Max King substantially different from that of Hymenaeus and Philetus (2 Timothy 2:14-19)?

> *2 Timothy 2:14-19 - ¹⁴Remind them of these things, and solemnly charge them in the presence of God not to wrangle about words, which is useless and leads to the ruin of the hearers. ¹⁵Be diligent to present yourself approved to God as a workman who does not need to be ashamed, accurately handling the word of truth. ¹⁶But avoid worldly and empty chatter, for it will lead to further ungodliness, ¹⁷and their talk will spread like gangrene. Among them are Hymenaeus and Philetus, ¹⁸men who have gone astray from the truth saying that the resurrection has already taken place, and they upset the faith of some. ¹⁹Nevertheless, the firm foundation of God stands, having this seal, "The Lord knows those who are His," and, "Everyone who names the name of the Lord is to abstain from wickedness." (NASB)*

Since the gospel is directly tied with the concept of the resurrection, why is the 70 A.D. doctrine not rightly identified as another gospel (Galatians 1:6-9)?

> *Galatians 1:6-9 - ⁶I am amazed that you are so quickly deserting Him who called you by the grace of Christ, for a different gospel; ⁷which is really not another; only there are some who are disturbing you and want to distort the gospel of Christ. ⁸But even if we, or an angel from heaven, should preach to you a gospel contrary to what we have preached to you, he is to be accursed! ⁹As we have said before, so I say again now, if any man is preaching to you a gospel contrary to what you received, he is to be accursed! (NASB)*

Because the proponents of realized eschatology advocate a different hope than the one set forth in Scripture (Acts 23:6; 24:14-15; 1 Corinthians 15:12-14; 1 Peter 1:3-5), we can no more have fellowship with them than with those who preach a different Lord, God, faith, or baptism (Ephesians 4:1-6).

> *Acts 23:6 - But perceiving that one group were Sadducees and the other Pharisees, Paul began crying out in the Council, "Brethren, I am a Pharisee, a son of Pharisees; I am on trial for the hope and resurrection of the dead!" (NASB)*

> *Acts 24:14-15 - [14]"But this I admit to you, that according to the Way which they call a sect I do serve the God of our fathers, believing everything that is in accordance with the Law and that is written in the Prophets; [15]having a hope in God, which these men cherish themselves, that there shall certainly be a resurrection of both the righteous and the wicked. (NASB)*

> *1 Corinthians 15:12-14 - [12]Now if Christ is preached, that He has been raised from the dead, how do some among you say that there is no resurrection of the dead? [13]But if there is no resurrection of the dead, not even Christ has been raised; [14]and if Christ has not been raised, then our preaching is vain, your faith also is vain. (NASB)*

> *1 Peter 1:3-5 - [3]Blessed be the God and Father of our Lord Jesus Christ, who according to His great mercy has caused us to be born again to a living hope through the resurrection of Jesus Christ from the dead, [4]to obtain an inheritance which is imperishable and undefiled and will not fade away, reserved in heaven for you, [5]who are protected by the power of God through faith for a salvation ready to be revealed in the last time. (NASB)*

> *Ephesians 4:1-6 - [1]Therefore I, the prisoner of the Lord, implore you to walk in a manner worthy of the calling with which you have been called, [2]with all humility and gentleness, with patience, showing tolerance for one another in love, [3]being diligent to preserve the unity of the Spirit in the bond*

of peace. ⁴There is one body and one Spirit, just as also you were called in one hope of your calling; ⁵one Lord, one faith, one baptism, ⁶one God and Father of all who is over all and through all and in all. (NASB)

CHAPTER 9
The Judge of All

As Creator of all things, and of man whom He created in His own image, God is also the source of all moral and covenant law. Abraham recognized Him as "the judge of all the earth" (Genesis 18:25). Isaiah spoke about His relation to the Jews, "For Jehovah is our judge . . . our lawgiver . . . our king" (Isaiah 33:22). He judged both individuals and nations, determining the use and destiny of each. His judgments would be always on the basis of righteousness and justice, for these are the foundation of His throne (Psalm 89:14; 97:2-3). When Jehovah seated Christ at His right hand and gave Him all authority in heaven and on earth, that included His role as judge over all that was involved in His kingship.

Jesus said that God sent Him not "to judge the world; but that the world should be saved through him" (John 3:17). However, though He judged no man (John 8:15), He said, "And yet if I judge"—if His teaching should bring men under judgment—"my judgment is true: for I am not alone, but I and the Father that sent me" (verse 16). It would be the Father's judgment through Him, a legal judgment at the mouth of at least two witnesses. Toward the close of His ministry Jesus repeated the fact that He did not judge, "And if any man hear my sayings, and keep them not, I judge him not: for I came not to judge the world, but to save the world" (John 12:47). He enlarged on this matter of judgment by saying, "He that rejecteth me, and receiveth not my words, hath one that judgeth him: the word that I have spoken, the same shall judge him in the last day" (verse 48) for *the word that He spoke was the word given to Him by the Father* (verses 49-50).

Observe that Jesus did not say, "All men shall be judged by the word that I spake,"—but, "If any man hear my sayings," those who were hearing Him and rejecting what He said would be judged by what he was saying. Men will be judged by the divine law under which they lived. All men, from Adam to the end of time, have and will continue to live under God's moral law. The Jews lived under the law of God through Moses by which they will be judged (Romans 2:12), and Christians live under the New Covenant of Christ, by which they will be judged. Jesus added, The word that I speak "shall judge him in the last day," the resurrection day.

Jesus said that those whom Cod gave Him would be raised "at the last day" (John 6:39). Jesus said the same thing concerning those who will have eternal life through belief in Him, "I will raise him up at the last day" (verse 40). Of the one drawn to Him by the Father, He affirmed, "I will raise him up in the last day" (verse 44); and of the one who should have eternal life by eating His flesh and drinking his blood, another way of saying, "he that believeth" (verse 47), "I will raise him up at the last day" (verse 40). Four times Jesus said that the righteous, *those having eternal life*, will be raised at or in the last day. If the righteous, those having eternal life are raised at the last day and those who rejected His word are judged in the last day (12:48), it follows that both will be raised and judged at the same point of time. *There will be no place for a thousand years between the two.*

Jesus foretold the day of judgment and the destruction of Jerusalem which would fulfill Daniel 9:7. His graphic description of the event is recorded in the first three Gospels. It will be a judgment executed by Himself, when they will "see the Son of Man coming on the clouds of heaven with power and great glory" (Matthew 24:30); *"clouds of heaven" is a **metaphorical description** of His coming with the Roman legion to destroy the city.* The destruction of the city and the temple was a judgment executed by the Son at the right hand of God. *Jesus made it clear that* **this had no reference to His final coming** *when He said, "This generation shall not pass away, till all these things be accomplished"* (Matthew 24:34).

This was to be a day of judgment on the whole Jewish system. It was brought to an end. It was neither a day of the resurrection of the righteous and the wicked, nor was it a day of judgment of either. It was a day of the judicial wrath of God in which His righteous judgment was executed in divine justice; the nation had reached a point where it was no longer worthy to continue, so He brought it to an end. The Jews will always exist as a people but never as a kingdom (Jeremiah 22:30; 30:11).

"Then," next in order of time, "shall the kingdom of heaven be likened unto . . ." (Matthew 25). Jesus continued by likening the kingdom to ten virgins, a man going into afar country and entrusting his goods to his servants, and concluded with His description of the final judgment. The King shall come with His holy angels; He shall sit "on the throne of his glory"; all the nations shall be gathered before Him; and He shall separate them into two groups, one on His right hand, and the other on His left. "Then shall the King say unto them on his right hand, Come, ye blessed of my Father, inherit the kingdom prepared for you from the foundation of the world" (verse 34). "Then shall he say also unto them on the left hand, Depart from me, ye cursed, into the eternal fire which is prepared for the devil and his angels" (verse 41). Jesus concluded, "And these shall go away into eternal punishment: but the righteous into eternal life"(verse 46). Remember Jesus said that this should be "at the last day"(John 6:39, etc). *To argue that is occurred at the destruction of Jerusalem, A.D. 70 is to ignore what Jesus said and the facts of the destruction of Jerusalem.* **This judgment is yet in the future.**

In their preaching that followed the day of Pentecost, the apostles emphasized a day of judgment to come in which Jesus Christ would be the judge. It would be God's judgment through His appointed judge. To the moralists of his day Paul spoke of the judgment of God as being according to truth (Romans 2:2). Did they think that they could escape that judgment if they lived in violation of moral truth (verse 3)? For the moralists it would be judgment by Jesus Christ the judge based on the universal moral law of God as set forth in Paul's gospel (verse 16). Furthermore, the judgment would be universal, one in which all would "stand before the judgment-seat of God," (Romans 14:10, 12; 2 Corinthians 5:10). On the basis of this universal judgment Paul called upon the heathen philosophers of Athens to repent; "Inasmuch as he hath appointed a day in which he will judge the world in righteousness by the man whom he hath ordained; whereof he hath given assurance unto all men, in that he hath raised him from the dead" (Acts 17:30-31). The resurrection of Jesus is God's guarantee that He has been exalted to the position of King and Judge of all men.

Paul described the resurrection of all men, as foretold by Jesus (John 5:28-29). It shall be accompanied by the Lord Himself, a shout, and the voice of the archangel; the dead in Christ shall rise first. "Then we that are alive, that are left, shall together-with them be caught up in the clouds, to meet the Lord in the air: and so shall we ever be with the Lord" (1 Thessalonians 4:13-17). Paul described the coming of the Lord as being with His angels, in flaming fire, executing vengeance on the wicked, but being glorified in His saints (2 Thessalonians 1:6-10). *But he hastened to say that the day of the Lord was not just at hand* (2 Thessalonians 2:1-2), **but that day is yet in the future.**

Peter wrote that the ancient world was destroyed by water, the flood in Noah's day, "But the heavens that now are, and the earth, by the same word have been stored up for fire, being reserved against the day of judgment and destruction of ungodly men" (2 Peter 3:6-7). Men may act as though God was slack in His promises and willfully forget the lessons of history and the word of God, but God's word is sure. Peter continued, "But the day of the Lord will come as a thief [*unannounced H.H.*] in the which the heavens shall pass away with a great noise, and the elements shall be dissolved with fervent heat, and the earth and the works that are therein shall be burned up" (verse 10). Beyond this, "we look for new heavens and a new earth, wherein dwelleth righteousness" (verse 13).

This brings the matter to the final battle between Satan and the seed of the woman. Satan is pictured as gathering together all the anti-God and anti-Christ forces of earth in a last furious effort to destroy the work of God. *One must remember that this is a great spiritual conflict*, not physical; it is worldwide, not local. The fire that came down out of heaven and devoured Satan's forces is a symbolic summary of the end brought about by the Lord, His coming in flaming fire as set forth in Matthew 25, 1 and 2 Thessalonians, and 2 Peter. *It is the end that ushers in the final Judgment.* The devil is cast into the lake of fire where he and all his allies and followers "shall be tormented day and night for ever and ever" (Revelation 20:7-10).

The conflict that began in the Garden of Eden has been long and bitter, but the victory is complete and final. The devil that began the effort to destroy God's purpose in the human family, who brought death and destruction into His world of life and beauty, is now in the lake of fire. The event to follow is the final judgment in which the Messiah/judge sits upon the throne executing the judgment.

Certainty that the prophets spoke from God and that their prophecies were fulfilled in Christ may be illustrated by the following: Archers from various walks of life and at different periods of time are selected and placed at varying distances from a special target. The time selected for them to shoot an arrow (or arrows) is at midnight with a cloudy overcast sky. Each is blindfolded and turned about several times before letting loose his arrow. The first shoots at about 1400 yards from the target; the second about 1000 yards, the third 830, the fourth 755, the fifth between 750 and 725, the sixth and seventh about 700, the eighth, ninth, and tenth between 600 and 550, the eleventh approximately 520, and the twelfth 440. Remember that all are blindfolded, each has been turned round a few times, and it is a dark moonless night. The light is turned on; each arrow has hit the bull's eye of the target. Remarkable! someone exclaims. No, it is more than remarkable, it is miraculous; the arrows were shot by inspiration of God and divinely directed. This illustrates the Messianic prophecies from Moses to Malachi and the fulfillment in Jesus the Son of God. Who can honestly consider the wonders of prophecy and not be fully convicted by their evidence that Jesus is the Christ, the Son of God, the Messiah of the prophets?

Let us close our study with John's description of the great scene: "Then I saw a great white throne and Him who sat upon it, from whose presence earth and heaven fled away, and no place was found for them. And I saw the dead, the great and the small, standing before the throne, and books were opened; and another book was opened, which is the book of life; and the dead were judged from the things which were written in the books, according to their deeds. And the sea gave up the dead which were in it, and death and Hades gave up the dead which were in them; and they were judged, every one of them according to their deeds. Then death and Hades were thrown into the lake of fire. This is the second death, the lake of fire. And if anyone's name was not found written in the book of life, he was thrown into the lake of fire." (Revelation 20:11-15 NASB)

When Adam and Eve sinned, they were driven from the garden of Eden and separated from the "tree of life." At the east of the garden God placed Cherubim, "and the flame of a sword which turned every way, to keep the way of the tree of life" (Genesis 3:24). This separated the two from the tree lest they eat of it and continue to live in their sinful state. Access to it would be restored through the victory of the seed of the woman, by which men would be reconciled to God and gain access to the tree of life in the new heaven and new earth (Revelation 21-22). Those who would continue to serve Satan in rebellion against God would now be cast into the lake of fire, the eternal fire, eternally separated from God and the tree of life with no possibility of ever having access to either. This terrifying thought should be a strong and impelling motive to move men to flee from the coming wrath of God by taking refuge in the redeeming Saviour.

God has done all that He can do for the human family. He chose the Jews, descendants of Abraham, developed them into a nation, delivered them from Egyptian bondage, gave them the good land of Canaan, and sent them into captivity when they rebelled beyond redemption. Then He brought them back, and settled them in their own land. They continued to rebel, but He sent His only begotten Son in an effort to bring them back to Himself, but they crucified Him. He did not give up. He sent the apostles with the gospel to them first, but they rejected it and continue to reject it. What more can He do? They rejected Him under a political rule, they rejected Him under a spiritual rule, and there remains only force but that cannot produce willing submission.

God's appeal is on the basis of love, not force. In the psalm quoted so often in this book, God said to His Son, "Thy people offer themselves willingly / In the day of thy power, in holy array" (Psalm 110:3). Force can never produce a willing subjection, nor can it produce holiness which is the array of the willing subject. Love dies under force. Neither God nor man can force anyone to respond willingly and to be holy unto God. Therefore, force cannot be considered. The principle that has always stood fast is, "We love, because he first loved us" (1 John 4:19).

God offers the same spiritual salvation and freedom to the Gentiles. There is therefore nothing more that God can do by sending Jesus to either group. For them, it is now or never. The next move is the final judgment. *Do not be deceived by the theories of men.* (Such as mentioned in this paper. Mgb)

Time and the present order will pass away; what follows is a new heaven and a new earth, and "the holy city Jerusalem coming down out of heaven from God" (Revelation 21), the description of which we leave for the student to read, comprehend, and imagine to the best of his ability. Suffice to say that it is a picture of the saints at home with the Lord, there to be with Him through out an incomprehensible eternity. This is the end of which Paul said…that God may be all in all" (1 Corinthians 15:24-28). Beyond that, all is another mystery to be revealed and made known in that eternity of the new heaven and new earth. **Amen! Praise God our Father and Jesus our Saviour and Lord!** [13]

---

[13] The Messiah of Prophecy by Homer Hailey, pages 271-277, Religious Supply, Inc., Louisville, KY 40213

(**NOTE:** My Christian brethren and sisters, now you know the extent of this heresy. You must rise up and take a stand for the truth every time you hear this false doctrine mentioned in your local congregations. That is each of our responsibilities; "test the spirits" that bring you this "other gospel" which is not another but a delusion of the mind of men. Amen! mgb)

Morris Bowers
September 01, 2009

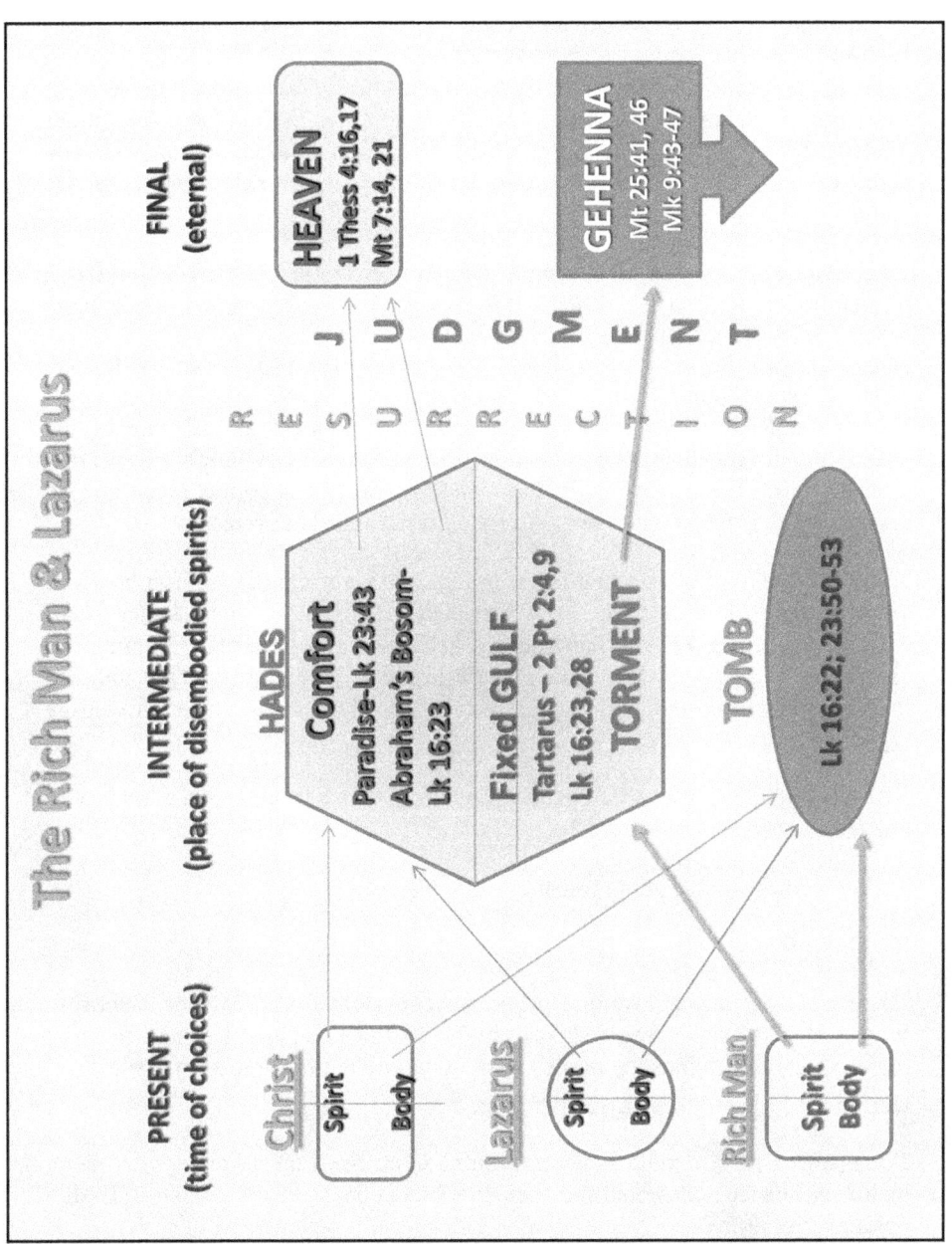

END NOTES

1- Copyright © 2007 by Wayne Petty. See Rights Notice below. This short paper is intended to be a very brief introduction to this view of "eschatology," or the study of "last events." As we mentioned in the introduction, most believers see these prophetic fulfillments to be yet future--a "futurist eschatology." This paper presents the most basic rudiments of the view that the fulfillments are in the past. This is called "preterist eschatology." The word "preterist" basically means "past."

It is our hope that this paper will simply stimulate readers to begin a re-examination of their convictions on this subject. It is a very broad study that will touch many aspects of our understanding of scripture.

But now our method of study will be different--and quite simple. Since Jesus placed His Return, the Resurrection, and the Judgment at the time of the destruction of Jerusalem, as we encounter these events in our Bible study, we will mentally "file" them accordingly. Now that the timeline is correct (according to Jesus Himself), the passages begin to fall into place and fit perfectly.

There is quite a lot of information regarding this view. One of the best books to set forth the position from the New Testament is *The Parousia,* by James Stuart Russell, written in 1878. ("Parousia" is a Greek word translated "coming" or "presence.") *The Parousia* may be read on-line at www.preteristarchive.com and may be ordered in book form at the International Preterist Association website www.preterist.org.

All Scripture quotations are from *The New King James Version,* unless otherwise indicated.

This essay is available at the website: *gospelthemes.com.*

Rights Notice

These electronically-transmitted pages are copyrighted © 2007 and belong to Wayne Petty. All rights reserved. You are free to download this electronic material for personal use, to make copies to share with others, or to mirror on your local web site, with the following restrictions:.

The material must remain intact and unmodified from the form supplied here, including header and footer and their graphics, copyright notice, the URL and postal addresses.

You may not charge for this material. If you have any questions about using this material, please contact the publisher at*gtp@gospelthemes.com.*

(Endnotes) 2- Sources

Archer, Gleason. 1982. *The Encyclopedia of Bible Difficulties*. Grand Rapids, MI: Zondervan.

Arndt, Wilbur and Gingrich, F. W. 1967. *A Greek-English Lexicon of the New Testament and Other Early Christian Literature*. Chicago, IL: University of Chicago.

Barbieri, Louis. 1983. Matthew. *The Bible Knowledge Commentary*. Wheaton, IL: Victor Books.

Camping, Harold. 1992. *1994?* New York, NY: Vantage Press.

Collett, Sidney. n.d. *All About The Bible*. London, England: Fleming H. Revell Co.

Edersheim, Alfred. 1957. *Sketches of Jewish Social Life in the Days of Christ*. Grand Rapids, MI: Eerdmans.

Foster, R. C. 1971. *Studies in the Life of Christ*. Grand Rapids, MI: Baker.

Geldenhuys, J. Norval. 1960. Luke. *The Biblical Expositor*. Vol. 3. Carl F. H. Henry, ed. Philadelphia, PA: A.J. Holman Co.

Kik, J. Marcellus. 1948. *Matthew Twenty-Four*. Philadelphia, PA: Presbyterian & Reformed.

King, Max. 1986. *The Cross and The Parousia of Christ*. Warren, OH: Parkman Road Church of Christ.

Jackson, Wayne. 2005. *The A.D. 70 Theory—A Review of the Max King Doctrine*. Stockton, CA: Courier Publications.

Lindsey, Hal. 1970. *The Late Great Planet Earth*. Grand Rapids, MI: Zondervan.

Lindsey, Hal. 1977. *Eternity*, January.

May, Cecil. 1984. Matthew 24. *The Biblical Doctrine of Last Things*. David Lipe, ed. Magnolia, MS: Magnolia Bible College.

McClintock, John and James Strong. 1969. *Cyclopedia of Biblical, Ecclesiastical, and Theological Literature*. Vol. 3. Grand Rapids, MI: Baker.

Scofield, C. I. 1945. *The Scofield Reference Bible*. New York, NY: Oxford Press.

Scott, J. B. 1975. Seventy Weeks. *The Zondervan Pictorial Bible Encyclopedia*. Vol. 5. Merrill Tenney, ed. Grand Rapids, MI: Zondervan.

Young, Edward J. 1954. Daniel. *The New Bible Commentary*. Davis, Stills, Kevan, eds. Grand Rapids, MI: Eerdmans.

(Endnotes) 3- Here is a listing of names and websites that you should visit as a study for yourselves:

Sam Dawson's web page is at www.gospelthemes.com

Wayne Petty's article is at
    http://www.gospelthemes.com/e-petty-pretintro.htm

Olan Hicks at www.theexaminer.org/volume6/number1/ad70.htm

Wayne Jackson,www.christiancourier.com/articles/read/jesus_foretells_the_coming_kingdom

Ed Stevens Email: preterist1@preterist.org
- Web Site: www.preterist.org

Mark Dunagan/Beaverton Church of Christ/503-644-9017
Mark's Email: mdunagan@easystreet.com
- Web Site: www.ch-of-christ.beaverton.or.us

Peter McPherson,
Web Site: http://www.peterboroughbibleproclaimer.ca
    http://www.hallvworthington.com/endworld.html#top

Don Preston's Preterist Research Institute: www.eschatology.org

William Bell's All Things Fulfilled: www.allthingsfulfilled.com

Mark Mayberry, Sermon preached at Woodland Hills in Conroe, TX, http://tinyurl.com/ad70doctrine   http://markmayberry.net/

The A.D. 70 Theory

More Bible workbooks that you can order from Spiritbuilding.com or your favorite Christian bookstore.

BIBLE STUDIES

Inside Out (Carl McMurray)
Studying spiritual growth in bite sized pieces
Night and Day (Andrew Roberts)
Comparing N.T. Christianity and Islam
We're Different Because..., w/Manual (Carl McMurray)
A workbook on authority and recent church history
From Beneath the Altar (Carl McMurray)
A workbook commentary on the book of Revelation
1 & 2 Timothy and Titus (Matthew Allen)
A workbook commentary on these letters from Paul
The Parables, Taking a Deeper Look (Kipp Campbell)
A relevant examination of our Lord's teaching stories
The Minor Prophets, Vol. 1 & 2, w/PowerPack (Matthew Allen)
Old lessons that speak directly to us today
Esteemed of God, the Book of Daniel, w/Manual (Carl McMurray)
Covering the man as well as the time between the testaments
Faith in Action: Studies in James (Mike Wilson)
Bible class workbook and commentary on James
The Lion is the Lamb (Andrew Roberts)
Study of the King of Kings, His glorious kingdom,
& His promised return
Church Discipline, w/Manual (Royce DeBerry)
A quarter's study on an important task for the church
Exercising Authority, w/Manual (John Baughn)
How we use and understand authority on a daily basis
Communing with the Lord (Matthew Allen)
A study of the Lord's Supper and issues surrounding it
Seeking the Sacred (Chad Sychtysz)
How to know God the way that HE wants us to know Him
1 Corinthians & 2 Corinthians study workbooks (Chad Sychtysz)
Detailed studies to take the student through these important letters
Living a Spirit Filled Life, w/PowerPack (Matthew Allen)
An overview study of Galatians & Ephesians with practical applications

TEENS/YOUNG ADULTS
Transitions, w/PowerPack (Ken Weliever)
A relevant life study for twenty-somethings changing age group
Snapshots: Defining Moments in a Girl's Life (Nicole Sardinas)
How to make godly decisions when it really matters
The Path of Peace (Cassondra Givans)
Relevant and important topics of study for teens
The Purity Pursuit (Andrew Roberts)
Helping teens achieve purity in all aspects of life
The Gospel and You (Andrew Roberts)
Thirteen weeks of daily lessons for Jr High and High School ages
Paul's Letter to the Romans (Matthew Allen)
Putting righteousness by faith on an understandable level

WOMEN
Reveal In Me... (Jeanne Sullivan)
A ladies study on finding and developing one's own talents
I Will NOT Be Lukewarm, w/PowerPack (Dana Burk)
A ladies study on defeating mediocrity
The Gospel of John (Cassondra Givans)
A study for women, by a woman, on this letter of John
Sisters at War (Cassondra Givans)
Breaking the generation gap between sisters in Christ
Will You Wipe My Tears? (Joyce Jamerson)
Resources to teach us how to help others through sorrow
Bridges or Barriers, w/Manual (Cindy DeBerry/Angie Kmitta)
Study encouraging harmony with younger/older sisters-in-Christ
Learning to Sing at Midnight (Joanne Beckley)
A study book about spiritual growth benefiting women of all ages
Forgotten Womanhood (Joanne Beckley)
Workbook which covers purity of purpose in serving God
Re-charging Your Prayer Life (Lonnie Cruse)
Workbook for any woman wanting a richer prayer life
Heading for Harvest (Joyce Jamerson)
A study to help ladies digest the fruit of the Spirit

PERSONAL GROWTH

Compass Points (Carl McMurray)
22 foundation lessons for home studies or new Christians
Marriage Through the Ages, w/Manual (Royce & Cindy DeBerry)
A quarter's study of God's design for this part of our life
Parenting Through the Ages, w/Manual (Royce & Cindy DeBerry)
Bible principles tested and explained by successful parents
What Should I Do?, w/Manual (Dennis Tucker)
A study that seeks Bible answers to life's important questions
When Opportunity Knocks, w/Manual (Matthew Allen)
Lessons on how to meet the JW/Mormon who knocks on your door

SPECIAL INTERESTS

In the Eye of the Hurricane - AUTISM (Juli Liske)
A family's journey from the shock of an autistic diagnosis to victory
I Cried Out, You Answered Me - DEPRESSION (Sheree McMillen)
What happens when faith and depression live in the same home
Her Little Soldier - DIABETES (Craig Dehut)
The journey of a young man suffering from Type 1 Juvenile Diabetes
For However Brief a Time (Warren Berkley)
A son's human interest tales of his father in a time now gone by
Family Bible Study Series (Ken Weliever)
A series of 16 quarters of Bible class curriculum ideas

JUST FOR KIDS

Greta's Purpose (Rebecca Helvey)
A children's book about a Great Dane who struggles with fitting in
Rudy's Path (Rebecca Helvey)
A story of a chocolate colored dog who finds belief, a family, and a name
Gus and Phil Stories Audio CDs (Ivan Benson)
Stories of true friendship and Christian values
Spiritbuilding Bible Challenge on CD (Mark Hudson, Alayne Hunt)
An entertaining CD-ROM series of Bible questions & answers
*All PowerPacks include PowerPoint presentations + Teacher's Manual

www.ingramcontent.com/pod-product-compliance
Lightning Source LLC
Chambersburg PA
CBHW031354040426
42444CB00005B/282